Advance Praise for *COVID-19 and the Future of Capitalism*

"This book is a major contribution to the study of capitalism in the time of the virus. All the new and the old contradictions meld into a major breakdown of the system. I strongly recommend this book."
— James Petras, professor emeritus of sociology, Binghamton University, New York

"Whenever a system is pushed towards and beyond the limits of its normal functioning, as is the case of capitalism today under these conditions, it generates forces that can be mobilized either towards the right or the left. The value and importance of this book is that it provides a clear and succinct analysis of these forces. I am not aware of any other book that analyses the dynamics of capitalist development as well in this conjuncture."

— Henry Veltmeyer, professor, Universidad Autónoma de Zacatecas, Mexico; professor emeritus, Saint Mary's University

D0224797

ALSO IN THE CRITICAL DEVELOPMENT STUDIES SERIES

COVID-19 and the Future of Capitalism

Postcapitalist Horizons Beyond Neoliberalism

EFE CAN GÜRCAN, ÖMER ERSIN
KAHRAMAN, AND SELEN YANMAZ

CRITICAL DEVELOPMENT STUDIES

Design: John van der Woude, JVDW Designs
Printed and bound in Canada

Published in North America by Fernwood Publishing
32 Oceanvista Lane, Black Point, Nova Scotia, B0J 1B0
and 748 Broadway Avenue, Winnipeg, Manitoba, R3G 0X3
www.fernwoodpublishing.ca

Published in the rest of the world by Practical Action Publishing
27a Albert Street, Rugby, Warwickshire CV21 2SG, UK

Fernwood Publishing Company Limited gratefully acknowledges the financial support of the Government of Canada through the Canada Book Fund and the Canada Council for the Arts, the Nova Scotia Department of Communities, Culture and Heritage, the Manitoba Department of Culture, Heritage and Tourism under the Manitoba Publishers Marketing Assistance Program and the Province of Manitoba, through the Book Publishing Tax Credit, for our publishing program.

Library and Archives Canada Cataloguing in Publication

Title: COVID-19 and the future of capitalism: postcapitalist horizons beyond neo-liberalism / Efe Can Gürcan, Ömer Ersin Kahraman and Selen Yanmaz.
Names: Gürcan, Efe Can, author. | Kahraman, Ömer Ersin, 1983- author. | Yanmaz, Selen, 1983- author.
Series: Critical development studies ; 6.
Description: Series statement: Critical development studies ; 6 | Includes bibliographical references and index.
Identifiers: Canadiana 20210139382 | ISBN 9781773632575 (softcover)
Subjects: LCSH: Capitalism—Forecasting. | LCSH: COVID-19 Pandemic, 2020-—Economic aspects. | LCSH: COVID-19 Pandemic, 2020-—Social aspects.
Classification: LCC HB501 .G87 2021 | DDC 306.3/42—dc23

Contents

Critical Development Studies Series

Three decades of uneven capitalist development and neoliberal globalization have devastated the economies, societies, livelihoods and lives of people around the world, especially those in societies of the Global South. Now more than ever, there is a need for a more critical, proactive approach to the study of global and development studies. The challenge of advancing and disseminating such an approach — to provide global and development studies with a critical edge — is on the agenda of scholars and activists from across Canada and the world and those who share the concern and interest in effecting progressive change for a better world.

This series provides a forum for the publication of small books in the interdisciplinary field of critical development studies — to generate knowledge and ideas about transformative change and alternative development. The editors of the series welcome the submission of original manuscripts that focus on issues of concern to the growing worldwide community of activist scholars in this field. Critical development studies (CDS) encompasses a broad array of issues ranging from the sustainability of the environment and livelihoods, the political economy and sociology of social inequality, alternative models of local and community-based development, the land and resource-grabbing dynamics of extractive capital, the subnational and global dynamics of political and economic power, and the forces of social change and resistance, as well as the contours of contemporary struggles against the destructive operations and ravages of capitalism and imperialism in the twenty-first century.

The books in the series are designed to be accessible to an activist readership as well as the academic community. The intent is to publish a series of small books (54,000 words, including bibliography, endnotes, index and front matter) on some of the biggest issues in the interdisciplinary field of critical development studies. To this end, activist scholars from across the world in the field of development studies and related academic disciplines are invited to submit a proposal or the draft of a book that conforms to the stated aim of the series. The editors will consider the submission of complete manuscripts within the 54,000-word limit. Potential authors are encouraged to submit a proposal that includes a rationale and short synopsis of the book, an outline of proposed chapters, one or two sample chapters, and a brief biography of the author(s).

Series Editors

HENRY VELTMEYER is a research professor at Universidad Autónoma de Zacatecas (Mexico) and professor emeritus of International Development Studies at Saint Mary's University (Canada), with a specialized interest in Latin American development. He is also co-chair of the Critical Development Studies Network and a co-editor of Fernwood's Agrarian Change and Peasant Studies series. The CDS *Handbook: Tools for Change* (Fernwood, 2011) was published in French by University of Ottawa Press as *Des outils pour le changement : Une approche critique en études du développement* and in Spanish as *Herramientas para el Cambio*, with funding from Oxfam UK by CIDES, Universidad Mayor de San Andrés, La Paz, Bolivia.

ANNETTE AURÉLIE DESMARAIS is the Canada Research Chair in Human Rights, Social Justice and Food Sovereignty at the University of Manitoba (Canada). She is the author of *La Vía Campesina: Globalization and the Power of Peasants* (Fernwood, 2007), which has been republished in French, Spanish, Korean, Italian and Portuguese, and *Frontline Farmers: How the National Farmers Union Resists Agribusiness and Creates our New Food Future* (Fernwood, 2019). She is co-editor of *Food Sovereignty: Reconnecting Food, Nature and Community* (Fernwood, 2010); *Food Sovereignty in Canada: Creating Just and Sustainable Food Systems* (Fernwood, 2011); and *Public Policies for Food Sovereignty: Social Movements and the State* (Routledge, 2017).

RAÚL DELGADO WISE is a research professor and director of the PhD program in Development Studies at the Universidad Autónoma de Zacatecas (Mexico). He holds the prestigious UNESCO Chair on Migration and Development and is executive director of the International Migration and Development Network, as well as author and editor of some twenty books and more than a hundred essays. He is a member of the Mexican Academy of Sciences and editor of the book series, Latin America and the New World Order, for Miguel Angel Porrúa publishers and chief editor of the journal *Migración y Desarrollo*. He is also a member of the international working group, People's Global Action on Migration Development and Human Rights.

Introduction

The coronavirus disease 2019 (COVID-19) pandemic has led to the most significant public health emergency of the twenty-first century, with enormous implications for global capitalism. Some forecasts suggest that the COVID-19 pandemic is likely to plunge the world economy into a deep-seated crisis whose consequences will be even worse than the Great Depression of the 1930s (Caşın 2020). These forecasts were validated by Gita Gopinath (2020), chief economist of the International Monetary Fund (IMF), who described the current situation as "the worst recession since the Great Depression, far worse than the Global Financial Crisis." The COVID-19 pandemic exposes the contradictions of neoliberal capitalism amidst the failure of global markets to provide adequate solutions to the global health crisis. This pandemic seems to have accelerated commodification and labour precarization with the push of digital and surveillance capitalism. Newly emerging patterns of online consumerism go hand in hand with the reinforcement of labour flexibility under conditions of understaffing as well as remote and diluted working. Adding to the complexity of the situation, the COVID-19 pandemic could not prevent the emergence and proliferation of social protests worldwide, from the Black Lives Matter (BLM) mobilization, the Paris protests against Emmanuel Macron's new national security bill, and Indian farmers' protests, to the anti-mask and anti-lockdown demonstrations. However, most of these protests have so far manifested themselves as dispersed "countermovements" in a Polanyian sense rather than as direct confrontations against capitalism (Polanyi 2001).

What is more, Western leaders' statements may well be interpreted as early signs of rapidly accelerating geopolitical turbulence and a crisis of the capitalist-imperialist system as a whole. German Chancellor Angela Merkel described the COVID-19 pandemic as the greatest threat since World War II. The European Union (EU), already suffering from heavy blows dealt by the 2009 European debt crisis and Brexit (Britain Exit), has been accused by Spanish Prime Minister Pedro Sanchez of abandoning his country. For similar reasons, Italian mayors have ripped down EU flags and politicians have participated in popular protests targeting the EU's indifferent attitude.

Meanwhile, Italy and Spain welcomed generous medical aid delivered by China and Russia. Italy, one of the top troop contributors to the North Atlantic Treaty Organization (NATO), went so far as to host Russian military personnel operating near a US military base (Braw 2020; Clark 2020; Smith 2020).

The cracks within the Atlantic Alliance seem to be accompanied by a rising Sinophobia. French President Emmanuel Macron openly targeted China with his statement: "There are clearly things that have happened that we don't know about" (Mallet and Khalaf 2020). During his term, former US President Donald Trump publicly supported claims that the pandemic originated in a lab in Wuhan and proclaimed that he had decided to defund the World Health Organization (WHO) for its "insidious relations with China" (Chomsky 2020). He insisted on branding COVID-19 as the "Chinese disease" (Viala-Gaudefroy and Lindaman 2020). Similarly, US Secretary of State Mike Pompeo directed open threats at China: "There will be a time when the people responsible will be held accountable.... There will be a time for assigning blame" (Bild 2020). Pompeo went so far as to name China "as the most dangerous adversary for the United States and for all Western governments." He added: "We're going to do the right things by building up our military" (Finnegan and Margolin 2020). British Foreign Secretary Dominic Raab joined the chorus by declaring: "We'll have to ask the hard questions about how it came about and how it couldn't have been stopped earlier.... We can't have business as usual after this crisis" (France 24 2020).

The aim of this book is two-fold: First, we offer a careful analysis of how the COVID-19 pandemic reveals and intensifies the contradictions of capitalism around areas that have been taking on greater salience. Second, we contribute to discussions on how to address these contradictions and transcend the limitations of global capitalism in the future. Our analysis relies on a Marxist framework, which is primarily concerned with the critique of capitalism and the study of social classes, with a strong emphasis on "exploitation (i.e., the appropriation of wealth), oppression (ideologically and politically based social exclusions and inequalities), and emancipation (the transcendence and abolition of class exploitation and oppression)" (Gürcan 2018: 3). Throughout the book, we strive to strike a balance between theory and practice by avoiding excessively abstract language while also not compromising analytical depth.

Chapter 1 examines the accelerated digitalization of global capitalism, which has been even further brought to the fore during the COVID-19 crisis. If the goal is really to understand the current transformations and future orientation of capitalism, then perhaps the best place to begin is with how capitalism renews itself and creates novel contradictions that leave their mark on social development. These developments are most apparent in the commodification of data, cyber-physical systems, and digital platforms, which are often glorified as the historic achievements of the Fourth Industrial Revolution (4IR) from a pro-capitalist and techno-optimistic standpoint. Grounded on a combined reading of "digital and surveillance capitalism," we assert that digitalization constitutes a crucial dynamic that drives both the crisis and renewal of global capitalism in the COVID-19 conjuncture as a defining moment of the capitalist system. While promising greater efficiency and flexibility for profit maximization, digitalization serves to intensify socioeconomic inequalities, consolidate the monopoly power of corporations, and impose new forms of surveillance and social control.

In Chapter 2, we extend our analysis to how the renewal of global capitalism to transcend its crisis tendencies finds its justification in the COVID-19 pandemic, which inaugurates a new phase of "disaster capitalism" through organized fear. This suggests that the pandemic serves as a medium for rejuvenating global capitalism by deploying a culture of fear that feeds its growth from catastrophic outcomes. We base our analysis on a historical framework of neoliberalism, whose development is owed to a political-economic and cultural context constructed around disasters. Our case studies address emblematic examples taken from the Pinochet coup in Chile, Argentina's military dictatorship era, "shock therapy" economics in Russia, and the US war on terror following 9/11. This historical framework helps us to conduct an anticipatory analysis of the post-COVID system of global capitalism shaped by a fear-driven rhetoric of disaster. Fear elements arisen from the COVID-19 conjuncture include not only health concerns but also far-right populisms and Sinophobia. Finally, our analysis revisits the theme of surveillance capitalism to emphasize how the COVID-19 disaster ends up fuelling the monopoly power of Big Tech.

Following the Marxist framework depicted above, Chapter 3 brings a labour perspective into our critical discussion of capitalism in the COVID-19 era. In this chapter, we provide a more-focused perspective on the implications of digital, surveillance and disaster capitalism for the working class. We proceed from the centrality of labour in the original formulations of capitalism in classical Marxism to argue that the current transformations of global capitalism give way to a new phase of "neoliberal labour regime" facilitated by the COVID-19 disaster. We underline that our production systems and industrial relations are not the sole objects of these transformations. The restructuring of the neoliberal labour regime, driven by digital (and surveillance) capitalism and accelerated by disaster capitalism, also shapes our private ways of life and social institutions. As such, increasing levels of labour flexibility and precarization are accompanied by increased surveillance and mass impoverishment in relative, if not absolute, terms. What is fundamentally in question here is that digital capitalism provides an enabling environment for record levels of surplus value extraction at the expense of material and psychological pauperization. Ultimately, we identify a minimum of seven mechanisms of labour-related insecurity accelerating pauperization and exploitation in the COVID-19 era: labour market insecurity, income insecurity, employment insecurity, job insecurity, skill reproduction insecurity, work insecurity, and representation insecurity.

Any ambitious attempt at a fuller understanding of global capitalism must accord due consideration to imperialism as a defining feature of the contemporary world system. The same goes for the task of unveiling the implications of the COVID-19 disaster for global capitalism. We thus maintain that any foundational attempt at understanding the COVID-19 era from a Marxist perspective necessitates an analysis of imperialism as much as that of labour relations. Against this backdrop, Chapter 4 turns the spotlight on to the rising relevance of imperialism in the COVID-19 era, particularly when it comes to the digital, ecological, medical, and geopolitical dimensions of the imperialist system. Our analysis explores the growing influence of Big Tech on US imperialism and hegemonic governance institutions at the expense of intensifying a "digital cold war." This adds to how the COVID-19 conjuncture serves to produce a "socioecological" and "technological" fix to the ongoing crisis of global capitalism with the pretext of environmental sustainability. As such, Western imperialism may be able to rejuvenate its global hegemony while using sustainability as a pretext to cut labour costs, worsen working conditions, and launch a new wave of "green" and "blue" grabbing. In the context of the pandemic, we also point to the increasing relevance of Big Pharma backed by imperialist states and "philanthropic" organizations from the Global North. An important consequence of this situation is the consolidation of the imperialist intellectual property rights and the intensification of international rivalry in health. Finally, and relatedly, the pandemic environment is conducive to global conflicts against the background of the intensification of geopolitical rivalries and increased multipolarity.

Building on the imperialism debate, Chapter 5 carries our discussion about the hegemonic renewal of global capitalism even further. We explore the two most popular proposals of capitalist reform that stand out in the COVID-19 era: the Great Reset and the Green New Deal. Both proposals express a desire to re-establish the credibility of global capitalism through socially and environmentally responsible reforms centred on the conception of "dollar-green capitalism." Key to this conception is accelerating the digitalization of capitalism and technological innovations by taking advantage of the COVID-19 conjuncture. The Great Reset proposal is put forth by the World Economic Forum (WEF), which is known as one of the most outspoken advocates of global capitalism. As for the Green New Deal, this proposal is represented by environmental Keynesianism, even though it appeals to a wide audience, including former war advocates from the Second Gulf War era, establishment liberals, and democratic socialists. The big government rhetoric of these proposals is essentially aimed at protecting capitalist interests through the method of "greenwashing" and does not involve a firm rejection of imperialism. Our analysis points to the need for an eco-socialist framework that puts forth democratic ecological planning alongside a well-planned nationalization and socialization agenda away from the profit motive.

In Chapter 6, we further develop our proposals based on a critical discussion of postcapitalist alternatives to green capitalism in the context of the COVID-19 pandemic. Our discussion identifies six major strategies that emanate from the postcapitalism debate: smashing capitalism, dismantling capitalism, taming capitalism, resisting capitalism, escaping capitalism, and, finally, eroding capitalism. We categorize the first three of these strategies under the non-revolutionist camp, which does not substantially differ from the reformism of green capitalism. Our critique proposes to go beyond reformism and considers that the deepening crisis of capitalism in the COVID-19 conjuncture may be read as an early warning sign of revolutionary situations to come. After discussing the non-revolutionist alternatives, we shift our attention to the strategies of resisting and escaping capitalism, whose prefigurative character impedes the implementation of meaningfully radical alternatives to revolutionize society. Despite the limits of such strategies, we observe how the pandemic period testifies to the revival of the solidarity economy and widescale social protests, such as the Black Lives Matter movement. In concluding our analysis, we suggest placing greater emphasis on the strategy of eroding capitalism, which is to be supplemented by a stronger tone of anti-imperialism and the struggle against monopoly capitalism. We maintain that this strategy promises long-term and far-reaching changes by combining revolutionary and state-led strategies with a social-economy approach.

Global capitalism has been undergoing a profound transformation over the last few decades, with digitalization and new surveillance mechanisms taking the lead in this process. On the one hand, the rise of digital and surveillance capitalism paves the way for unprecedented capabilities to maximize corporate profits through greater efficiency and flexibility by commodifying and instrumentalizing digital technologies. On the other, this development creates sharpening contractions that manifest themselves in the widening of socioeconomic inequalities and the rise of digital monopolies, which have gained the ability to colonize our lives by commodifying every form of data.

This being said, the digitalization of capitalism has acquired new momentum with the onset of the COVID-19 pandemic. With this pandemic, global capitalism has been provided with a historic opportunity to renew itself away from the current structural crisis by accelerating digitalization and the rise of new surveillance mechanisms. Put differently, the pandemic is instrumentalized by global capitalism to take advantage of the fear environment created by the catastrophic consequences of the pandemic for a new period of capitalist expansion. In a way to invalidate techno-optimistic accounts about the miracles of digital capitalism, however, this expansion takes place at the expense of the working class, which testifies to the restructuring of the neoliberal labour regime in a direction to intensify labour flexibility and precarization at unprecedented levels.

Another important consequence of the current transformations of capitalism is the rise in relevance of imperialism in a new context. The growing influence of Big Tech creates an enabling environment for an all-out "capital, trade and technology war," with serious implications for labour and the environment. In the meantime, the backing of imperialist states and Western philanthropic institutions serves to advance the interests of Big Pharma to launch a new wave of privatization in global health. This imperialist vision is expected to draw its hegemonic legitimacy from global reforms, which are referred to with several names, including the Great Reset and the Green New Deal, as an expression of some form of green capitalism disguising the corporate intent behind an environmentally responsible "big government" rhetoric. Instead, we propose a "transitional program" to build socialism, which starts with a minimum program of achievable demands towards universal emancipation, i.e., a postcapitalist strategy of eroding capitalism. Any meaningful and long-term change away from capitalism requires the combination of revolutionary and state-led strategies with a social-economy approach, without losing sight of the anti-imperialist agenda.

REFERENCES

Bild. 2020. "Bild Interview with US Secretary of State Pompeo 'There Will Be a Time for Assigning Blame.'" *Bild*, April 13. <https://www.bild.de/politik/international/bild-international/mike-pompeo-on- bild-live-china-will-be-liable-for-the-damage-done- by-coronavirus-70022820.bild.html>.

Braw, E. 2020. "Beware of Bad Samaritans." *Foreign Policy*, March 30. <https://foreignpolicy.com/2020/03/30/russia-china-coronavirus- geopolitics/>.

Caşın, M.H. 2020. "US-China Virus Clash Could Escalate Into Hot War, Expert Warns." *Anadolu Ajansı*, April 18. <https://www.aa.com.tr/en/latest-on-coronavirus-outbreak/uschina-virus-clash-could-escalate-into-hot-war-expert-warns/1809536>.

Chomsky, N. 2020. "Gangster in the White House: Noam Chomsky on COVID-19, WHO, China, Gaza and Global Capitalism." *Democracy Now*, April 17. <https://www.democracynow.org/2020/4/17/noam_chomsky_coronavirus_trump_gaza_palestine>.

Clark, R. 2020. "Spain and Italy Have Been Abandoned by the EU." *Spectator*, April 1. <https://www.spectator.co.uk/article/spain-and-italy-have-been-abandoned-by-the-eu>.

Finnegan, C., and J. Margolin. 2020. "Pompeo Changes Tune on Chinese Lab's Role in Virus Outbreak, as Intel Officials Cast Doubt." *ABC News*, May 8. <https://abcnews.go.com/Politics/pompeo-tune-chinese-labs-role-virus-outbreak-intel/story?id=70559769>.

France 24. 2020. "Macron Voices Scepticism Over China's Handling of Covid-19 Outbreak." *France 24*, April 17. <https://www.france24.com/en/20200417-france-emmanuel-macron-covid-19-pandemic-china>.

Gopinath, G. 2020. "The Great Lockdown: Worst Economic Downturn Since the Great Depression." *IMF Blog*, April 14. <https://blogs.imf.org/2020/04/14/the-great-lockdown-worst-economic-downturn-since-the-great-depression/>.

Gürcan, E.C. 2018. "Theorizing Food Sovereignty from a Class-Analytical Lens: The Case of Agrarian Mobilization in Argentina." *Agrarian South: Journal of Political Economy*, 7, 3: 1–31.

Mallet, V., and R. Khalaf. 2020. "FT Interview: Emmanuel Macron Says It Is Time to Think the Unthinkable." *Financial Times*, April 16. <https://www.ft.com/content/3ea8d790-7fd1-11ea-8fdb-7ec06edeef84>.

Polanyi, K. 2001. *The Great Transformation: The Political and Economic Origins of Our Time*. Boston: Beacon Press.

Smith, O. 2020. "Anti-EU Fury: Italian Mayors Rip Down EU Flags in Outrage as Row with Brussels Intensifies." *Express*, April 5. <https://www.express.co.uk/news/world/1264946/EU-coronavirus-fury-flag-Brussels-Italy-European-Union-aid-latest-news>.

Viala-Gaudefroy, J., and D. Lindaman. 2020. "Donald Trump's 'Chinese Virus': The Politics of Naming." *The Conversation*, April 21. <https://theconversation.com/donald-trumps-chinese-virus-the-politics-of-naming-136796>.

① The Rise of Digital Capitalism

Challenges Before and After COVID-19

As the COVID-19 pandemic unfolded around the globe and resulted in lockdowns and social isolation in many countries, life as we know it has been carried largely over to the digital world. This transition to the *new normal* has not only included regular activities of everyday life, such as work, education, and grocery shopping, but also many others, such as academic conferences, exercise, art lessons, museum visits and music festivals, to give a few examples. These activities started to be carried out through various popular digital channels, such as Blackboard for online classes, Microsoft Teams for remote working, Amazon Fresh for online grocery shopping, Zoom for social gatherings, and Google Arts & Culture for art events, among many others used worldwide, not to mention common social networking platforms, such as Facebook, Instagram and YouTube, serving a variety of needs. While the utilization of many of these channels and their technological infrastructure are not new to the COVID-19 context, the pandemic has massively accelerated their use in intensified and novel ways, to the point where they, in certain instances, became the only solution to carry on everyday activities. In the end, the pandemic period has shown the extent to which digital technologies have already been integrated, not merely into our economy but also to our physical, social, and cultural world in a rather ultra-capitalist form.

In this chapter, we scrutinize the accelerated digitalization of global capitalism in three sections. The first provides the historical background of digital capitalism against the backdrop of the Fourth Industrial Revolution (4IR), during which global capitalists took advantage of extreme automation and hyperconnectivity to initiate a new phase of commodification and capital accumulation. In the second section, we elaborate on what came to be called "digital capitalism" and its growing salience in the COVID-19 period. Global capitalism has been undergoing deep-rooted transformations whose defining effects can be seen in the accelerated commodification of data, the adoption of cyber-physical systems, and the platformication of the economy, especially in the context of the COVID-19 pandemic. These effects point to new opportunities for profit maximization and capital accumulation. In the third section, we delve into digital capitalism by problematizing the perspectives that celebrate its alleged potential to enhance efficiency and flexibility for businesses. Our analysis underlines how digital capitalism has initiated a new phase of monopolization, control, and surveillance, which ends up intensifying inequalities and enhancing the corporate power at unprecedented levels.

The Fourth Industrial Revolution as the Defining Moment of Global Capitalism

A word of caution is warranted before beginning to explore the historical background of digital capitalism. Our analysis does not proceed from a techno-determinist argument which suggests that the transformation of capitalism is primarily driven by technological changes (Clément 2015: 145). Notably, one should take into account the fact that technological development itself "is invariably a function of the level of science, the laws of a country, the policies of a regime, consumer demand, and much else" (Ollman 1971: 7). What is more, the transformation of global capitalism greatly owes to managerial practices facilitated by technology, which cannot be reduced to "some pure effect of the devices themselves" (Wajcman 2015: 95). This implies that capitalism constitutes a societal formation prone to instrumentalizing technology for profit maximization and capital accumulation purposes (Chandler and Fuchs 2019: 9–10). When addressing "platform capitalism," for example, we are not exclusively dealing with platform technologies per se, but rather with the nature of social relations and organizations that both enact and are enacted in the platform environment. Moreover, the growing salience of platform technologies and how they are deployed by corporate entities depend on certain ideological constructs that legitimize digital capitalism as an important dimension of contemporary capitalism (Chandler and Fuchs 2019). Therefore, studying the historical background of contemporary capitalism requires careful consideration of how the industrial revolutions have been instrumentalized under capitalism and what kind of social relations capitalism brings to the fore.

In the development of capitalism, each industrial revolution marked a historical turn for the global economy as reference points, where the new technological advancements were instrumentalized to maximize profits and capital accumulation. The three industrial revolutions before the 4IR were characterized by the introduction of steam power, electricity, and information communication technologies (ICTs), primarily to the production process (Schwab 2016; Philbeck and Davis 2018; Tan and Shang-Su 2017; Pollitzer 2018). The First Industrial Revolution, dating back to the 18th-century UK, led to the introduction of steam power into the manufacturing process and mechanized production, creating a massive increase in productivity levels. This period witnessed the transition from hand manufacturing to factory production as well as the growth of regional and global market economies and urbanization, which were essentially driven by increasing productivity and facilitated by developments in communication and transportation systems (Heller 2011).

The Second Industrial Revolution, dating from the mid-19th century to World War I, embraced the introduction of electric power and mass production systems with the application of the assembly line in conveyor production, "coalesc[ing] around the modern belief that science and technology are the way forward to a better life and that progress is in many ways a destiny for humanity" (Philbeck and Davis 2018: 19). During this time, technical and engineering knowledge was applied to the production process to ensure efficiency, standardization, speed, and precision (Pozdnyakova et al. 2019: 14). For instance, Henry Ford adapted Frederick Winslow Taylor's principles of scientific management to the production process and applied the assembly line in his automotive plant in 1913. Heavy industry, through large machine production, took the lead in economic development with the widescale adoption of Fordist strategies. These societal arrangements, facilitated by technology, led to "deep changes in the technical and organizational system: the growth of concentration of production and centralization of capital, creation of joint-stock companies and monopolies, and increase of the level of collectivization of labor" (Pozdnyakova et al. 2019: 14).

With the deployment of technological developments such as the telephone, telegraph, phonograph, cinema, cars and airplanes along capitalist interests, mass communication and transportation accelerated the interdependence and interaction of different parts of the world. Advertising assumed a key role in the marketing of mass-produced products, which eventually gave way to the emergence of a consumer society (Pozdnyakova et al. 2019). Large numbers of workers were gathered in factories for deskilled work, "with relatively permanent jobs, high wages, and guaranteed pensions" (Srnicek 2017: 15). This period also witnessed the emergence of a cognitive workforce, including scholars, engineers, and technicians.

The Third Industrial Revolution, which dates to World War II, "is usually called the computer or digital revolution because it was catalysed by the development of semiconductors, mainframe computing (1960s), personal computing (1970s and 80s) and the internet (1990s)" (Schwab 2016: 11). Starting with the 1970s, new ICTs were used for a rapid transition to post-Fordist social arrangements faced with the crisis of Fordist capitalism. These arrangements allowed greater flexibility in production and consumption, including mass customization. Vertically organized bureaucratic firms that characterize the Fordist era were gradually replaced by a system of networks and alliances that are horizontally organized and globally distributed. By deploying new technologies to advance a post-Fordist agenda, global capitalism also transformed the global division of labour by shifting production to the Global South, particularly countries allowing for lowest paying, most insecure, and unsafe sweatshop labour (Kobrin 1998):

> This process ... accelerated the outsourcing tendency initiated in the 1970s, when coordination costs were drastically cut as global communication and supply chains became easier to build and manage. Companies pushed more and more of their components outwards and Nike became an emblem of the lean firm: branding and design were managed in the high-income economies, while manufacturing and assembly were outsourced to sweatshops in the low-income economies. (Srnicek 2017: 18)

In the Global North, post-Fordist arrangements led to the decline of blue-collar manufacturing jobs through strategies favouring automation, atypical employment, and outsourcing. The axis of business profits shifted from production to development, design, and marketing (Pozdnyakova et al. 2019). This went hand in hand with an all-out state assault on unions (Srnicek 2017). With the growing commercialization of the internet in the late 1990s, moreover, the telecommunications sector and financial capital adopted a mutually empowering relationship. In this period, "when this [financial] sector was at its height, nearly 1 per cent of US gross domestic product (GDP) consisted of [venture capital] invested in tech companies; and the average size of [venture capital] deals quadrupled between 1996 and 2000" (Srnicek 2017: 17).

Eventually, the societal arrangements of capitalism in the era of the Third

Industrial Revolution paved the way for the Fourth Industrial Revolution by rapidly commodifying data and digital technologies. First coined by World Economic Forum founder and executive chair Klaus Schwab, the term 4IR is used here to refer to a historical landmark in the development of productive forces, where global capitalism instrumentalizes new technological developments to reshape social norms and political attitudes to economic development and international relations (Philbeck and Davis 2018). Facilitated by extreme automation and hyperconnectivity, this revolution perpetuates a new conception of the economy where the digital world is now taken for granted and new technologies "are becoming more integrated into our physical, social, and political spaces, altering behaviours, relationships, and meaning" (Philbeck and Davis 2018: 18).

The term 4IR has a much more encompassing meaning than Industry 4.0, where digital technologies are applied to manufacturing systems. It also includes technologies such as digital identification, artificial intelligence (AI), machine learning, autonomous vehicles, machine vision, advanced imaging, 3D printing, low-cost sensors, advanced robotics, new smart materials, genetic modification, cryptocurrencies depending on distributed ledger technologies, and the "internet of things" (IoT). These commodified technologies are nowadays being deployed to further capitalist interests by establishing a never-before-seen link between our physical/biological worlds and the digital world, where they can realize their potential to influence our physiological condition and cognitive faculties (Philbeck and Davis 2018). Moreover, digital technologies are used to generate new patterns of consumerism by allowing capitalists to anticipate and even determine our needs: "The day when [AI and IoT] finally meet, our everyday household appliances will not only interface with each other, as they do now, but will actually be able to foresee our preferences and tastes even before we realise we had them" (Tan and Shang-Su 2017: 6).

The IoT, which is a collection of software applications, sensors, and communication modules, make constant and readily available information about physical systems obtainable, which not only include systems of manufacturing but living ones, including the human body: "The big transformational promise of 4IR is in cyber-physical systems that will merge different digital technologies and integrate them within the physical, digital, and biological spheres. This will produce deep and systemic societal changes at a larger scale and a more rapid rate than previously seen" (Pollitzer 2018: 76). The blurring of the lines between digital, physical, and biological worlds, the continuous, easy, and cheap collection of data, the constant hyperconnectivity between various actors, automation of many practices through new technologies, and the resulting flexibility, speed, and efficiency of various activities imply that we have reached a new era of digital capitalism.

The Rise of Digital Capitalism

Digital capitalism can be understood as an increasingly salient dimension of contemporary capitalism representing "businesses that increasingly rely upon information technology, data, and the internet for their business models [which] cut across traditional sectors — including manufacturing, services, transportation, mining, and telecommunications — and [are], in fact, becoming essential to much of the economy today" (Srnicek 2017: 10). This definition underlines the fact that today's businesses develop a stronger dependence on the infrastructure provided by digital technologies and the legitimizing discourse of digital capitalism. Digital infrastructure here has to do with the use of a variety of technological tools ranging from those as fundamental as cell phones, tablets, and computers to relatively newer and more complicated ones, such as 3D printing, autonomous vehicles, and advanced robotics. Moreover, it encompasses the economy's increasing dependence on connectivity, which is primarily provided by the internet and the rise of the digital platforms offering business-to-business and business-to-customer solutions, such as data collection, storage, and analysis, online commerce, marketing and sales, personal and commercial computing, media and entertainment, and automation at various levels. At the ideological level, the use of digital technologies is justified based on a discourse that positively views digital capitalism as the ultimate economic model of productive efficiency, connectivity, cost-effectiveness, and flexibility (Fuchs 2015). This ideology also propagates an individualistic and consumerist idea that the corporate model allows for a high degree of freedom by allowing its users to freely "communicate, create, consume, and share" while concealing how the corporate control of digital technologies accelerates the commodification of every sphere of social life and labour precarity (Fuchs 2015: 293).

The term "digital capitalism" is also used to imply that data and information have become the dominant form of commodity and a key determinant of economic power. As Srnicek puts it, data today constitute "the [major] raw material that must be extracted, and the *activities* of the users [are] the natural source of this raw material" (2017: 28, emphasis in original). While the collection of data is not entirely new to capitalist businesses practices, one could observe today a qualitative leap forward in the speed, accessibility, and amount of data that can be collected at a much lower cost (Srnicek

2017; Watson 2020):

> As the internet expanded and firms became dependent on digital communications for all aspects of their business, data became increasingly relevant.... Data have come to serve a number of key capitalist functions: they educate and give a competitive advantage to algorithms; they enable the coordination and outsourcing of workers; they allow for the optimisation and flexibility of productive processes; they make possible the transformation of low-margin goods into high-margin services; and data analysis is itself generative of data, in a virtuous cycle. Given the significant advantages of recording and using data and the competitive pressures of capitalism, it was perhaps inevitable that this raw material would come to represent a vast new resource to be extracted from. (Srnicek 2017: 29)

Digitalization generates intensified connectivity between various systems, physical, biological, and digital, where data are constantly exploited by capitalist firms in the most "efficient" ways, with minimal disruption. This includes the creation of cyber-physical systems (CPS), which enable flexibility and agility in physical production through constant data collection and allow producers to answer to continuously changing market conditions, allowing for maximum mass customization, personalization, and efficiency. Similar systems are used with the human body, for example in the healthcare sector, where patients can be tracked for precise diagnosis and to improve treatment efficiency (Chou 2018). "With more relevant data for the patient, more effective preventive medicine can be practiced to reduce the overall cost of healthcare.... Traditional physical medical systems of all scales can be digitally transformed into CPS medical systems to improve their precision, flexibility, and agility" (2018: 111). Other sectors that are compatible with cyber-physical systems include transportation, where physical resources, such as cars, can be shared to create allegedly more "environmentally friendly" and "cost-effective" models (Chou 2018).

The COVID-19 pandemic has further amplified the adaptation of new technological advancements to capitalism. Particularly, the pandemic conditions encouraged a wide range of measures from lockdowns to social isolation and social distancing, which are conceived to be the most effective strategies to prevent the spread of the virus. The lessening of physical activities to a large extent led everyday practices to be carried over to the digital world, including but not limited to remote working and online education. Businesses rapidly initiated or amplified their digitalization efforts. Moreover, the pandemic conditions led to a massive increase in e-commerce, including online grocery shopping and the widespread use of digital media and entertainment products and services. As such, the COVID-19 pandemic brought new momentum to the digitalization of the economy under the *new normal*, with long-term implications for businesses, customers, and workers.

With the implementation of social isolation and distancing measures, many businesses initially saw an immense decline in consumer demand as individuals were advised to avoid any non-essential activities or interactions that would require physical contact. Sectors and services such as travel, transportation, restaurants, retail, theme parks, concert halls and clubs were among those that took the hardest hit from these measures. For instance, within the travel sector, airline, hotel, cruise, and rental car purchases have dropped radically, also affecting travel booking sites such as Expedia, Airbnb and Priceline. Similarly, there was a massive decline in the sales of services that offer ride-sharing, like Uber and Lyft, as well as the use of taxis and mass transit (Leatherby and Gelles 2020). Some of these sectors, such as travel, lodging, and entertainment, are expected to recover once the pandemic risk is minimized. However, this does not mean that all companies hurt by the pandemic will be able to recover. Yet in other cases, such as the retail industry, what is observed during the pandemic is an intensified manifestation of existing trends, where they were already unable to compete with the rise of e-commerce and discount brands (Leatherby and Gelles 2020). For instance, by March 2020, "Macy's, which said the cuts would affect the 'majority' of its 125,000 workers, lost most of its sales after the pandemic forced it to close stores. Gap, which also owns Old Navy and Banana Republic, said it would furlough nearly 80,000 store employees in the United States and Canada" (Maheshwari and Corkery 2020: para. 2). Indeed, while those businesses that offer digital products or services may have thrived during the pandemic, those that experimented with and invested in digitalization, before or at least during the pandemic, had a relatively easier time navigating the crisis (LaBerge et al. 2020).

A McKinsey and Company Global Survey in 2020, conducted with nearly 900 business executives across regions, industries, company sizes, and functional specialities shows that those companies "have accelerated the digitization of their customer and supply-chain interactions and of their internal operations by three to four years. And the share of digital or digitally enabled products in their portfolios has accelerated by a shocking seven years" (LaBerge et al. 2020: 2). The survey shows that the extent of companies' investment in digitalization created a significant difference in terms of revenue growth:

> At the organizations that experimented with new digital technologies during the crisis, and among those that invested more capital expenditures in digital technology than their peers did, executives are twice as likely to report outsize revenue growth than executives at other companies. (LaBerge et al. 2020: 7)

Similarly, a Digital Business Research study conducted by technology service company IDG Communications in 2019 with over 700 respondents from CIO, Computerworld, CSO, InfoWorld, and Network World site visitors as well as invited audiences, shows that there is an apparent link between digitalization and revenue growth (PwC 2020). With the adaptation of remote-working practices, the companies which already utilized collaboration technologies were able to continue their business operations for the most part. Similarly, those that utilized security measures such as multifactor authentication and sufficient VPN licences were able to protect sensitive information. The companies that invested in expanding their internet and network capacities also had an easier time maintaining the connections between various stakeholders and customers (Caldwell and Krishna 2020).

A striking example of the benefits of technological preparedness can be seen in the healthcare sector. The natural focus on safety, cleanliness, and health during the pandemic generated economic opportunities for various healthcare companies. As the pandemic created an increased need for personal protective equipment (PPE), such as masks, gloves and gowns, many companies were able to change their manufacturing processes to produce these PPE and other medical supplies. This easy and fast transition by many companies, including BYD, Gree, and Foxconn, would not be possible without the digitalization of business operations, such as management of resources and the labour force as well as high-level automation, including technologies such as digital design and 3D printing (PwC 2020). Moreover, digitalization of healthcare services, such as telemedicine and remote diagnostics, for instance, were used in the US to alleviate the workload of hospitals while helping patients stay socially isolated (BDO 2020).

Perhaps more interestingly, the aforementioned McKinsey and Company survey findings suggest that the pandemic conditions radically changed the way executives evaluate the role of digital technologies in business (LaBerge et al. 2020). Half of them stated that, regarding the application of these technologies, cost-saving was the priority before the pandemic. However, now, for more than half, investment in these technologies is seen as an opportunity to create a competitive advantage (LaBerge et al. 2020: 7). They saw technology capabilities as the key to success during the crisis. Digitalization is thus regarded as a long-term strategy by the executives, pointing to permanent transformation in business practices rather than short-term crisis management. For instance, in February 2020, China launched its New Infrastructure campaign, which focuses on the digital economy and innovation. The project includes investments in technologies such as "5G networks, big data centres, internet of things (IoT), blockchain, industrial automation, inter-city transit systems, high-voltage energy transmission, smart transportation and electric vehicle charging stations" (PwC 2020: 3). These developments are expected to make China the largest 5G market in the world, creating incentives for businesses working in related areas, such as telecom, smart manufacturing, smart cities, and data analytics (PwC 2020).

As the pandemic continued, many sectors, including telemedicine, online education, online gaming, and information technology (IT) services supporting remote working, saw exponential increases in demand. Companies developed innovative solutions to provide products and services. "For example, in March, over 30 financial institutions in China worked with an international leading payment platform to roll out 'contactless wealth management' products for customers. Property companies also changed their approach by using Artificial Intelligence (AI), Virtual Reality (VR), live streaming, and internet celebrities to sell apartments online" (PwC 2020: 2). Other examples include the digitalization of customer service, greater use of self-service, and contactless delivery (BDO 2020). A major transformation took place in terms of the transition to omnichannel commerce, specifically a shift towards e-commerce. There was an acceleration in digital consumption both in terms of the utilization of digital channels to satisfy consumer needs and in terms of the consumption of digital products and services. With limited access to physical shopping opportunities, customers turned to online channels, including those who had reservations about such platforms. Especially, grocery delivery services, such as Instacart, have gained popularity, where customers can easily satisfy their needs through a convenient app and utilize delivery services like curbside pick-up (BDO 2020).

Therefore, the use of online and on-demand platforms has increased. Consumers have also turned to digital content for entertainment. According to Statista data, COVID-19 has led 51% of internet users worldwide to utilize streaming services more than before. In the first three months of 2020,

Netflix received 16 million sign-ups (BDO 2020). Video game companies like Twitch and Nintendo and streaming services like Spotify are enjoying greater spending on their services (Leatherby and Gelles 2020). This platformification trend is not limited to those companies that provide digital content but also includes institutions and organizations of other types. For instance, live and pre-recorded virtual fitness classes are being streamed online as a solution to physical distancing. Moreover, all around the world, schools across all grades are carried on online platforms. Even the New York Stock Exchange has opted for online trading. While some of these organizations will return to traditional methods once the pandemic risk is minimized, others may offer hybrid models to utilize digitalization to their benefit (BDO 2020). Platforms have thus emerged as a critical business model that shares a big part of the digital workload during the pandemic.

Problematizing Digital Capitalism in the COVID Era: Big Tech and Surveillance

Corporate capabilities enhanced by digital technologies are celebrated in various ways. For businesses, these technologies are thought to provide more efficient, faster, more flexible, and less expensive solutions in production and delivering services. Businesses can opt for greater automation for activities in place of human labour and thus increase speed, reduce cost, and focus on profit-maximizing activities. They can become adaptable and ready to act fast in case of crisis and other abrupt changes in an agility advantage (Chou 2018; BDO 2020). Thus the "organizations that embrace digital solutions have greater resiliency in the face of adversity — and a leg up on the competition that will enable them to recover faster and pivot from playing defense to chasing growth" (BDO 2020: 3). More importantly, digitalization is believed to allow businesses to extract and utilize customer data to understand customer demand and needs better. They can act on more informed decisions thanks to greater data availability, which, in turn, amplifies the intended effects of the aforementioned solutions, making them smarter, more accurate, and precise.

From the customers' perspective, products and services can be mass customized and personalized, better satisfying their expectations, making consumption more attractive and convenient. Moreover, consumption becomes easier for the customer to the extent that the emphasis of consumption is shifting from the ownership of the product to the intended outcome of the product, through the sharing of physical resources for various services, such as the efficient distribution of access to mobility by Uber, which reduces the need for car ownership (Chou 2018). Thus, digitalization is celebrated for generating environmentally friendly solutions through efficiency and reduced use of physical resources. From a labour perspective, digitalization is much praised for automation, where machines can be utilized "to perform tasks that humans did not want to undertake or were not good at, preserving more favorable labor tasks for humans" (Chou 2018: 113). A case in point is how digitalization enables remote working and thus reduces health risks to employees by minimizing face-to-face interaction with each other and the customers, especially in the COVID-19 context. Furthermore, it decreases physical footprints and thus provides an environmentally friendly option (LaBerge et al. 2020). Digital capitalism also supposedly gives the employees better use of their time by providing flexibility. It is further argued that with remote working "digital collaboration is improving in leaps and bounds, both in terms of the sophistication of the tools to facilitate it and workers' level of comfort with it," preparing them better for a future where work revolves around these technologies (BDO 2020: 4). Remote working also provides the companies with a productivity advantage where "their employees [are] set up to work remotely [and so] their focus [can be] on leveraging collaboration technology and tools to maximize workforce productivity and sustain company culture" (BDO 2020: 3).

Rather than taking the benefits of digital capitalism at face value, it is important to take a closer look at the societal costs of such changes. Moving away from techno-optimistic accounts of digitalization, one could observe that the most basic premises of the capitalist economic system, where businesses seek "out new avenues for profit, new markets, new commodities, and new means of exploitation," are left intact (Srnicek 2017: 9). These conditions thereby lead to inhumane and unjust practices, especially in terms of labour. It follows that the digital transformation of today's capitalist economy responds to the fundamental needs of economic agents under the capitalist system, who seek to reduce production costs in relation to prices, mainly through the "adoption of efficient technologies and techniques in the labour process, specialisation, and the sabotage of competitors" (Srnicek 2017: 14).

As Srnicek argues, "capitalism, when a crisis hits, tends to be restructured. New technologies, new organisational forms, new modes of exploitation, new types of jobs, and new markets all emerge to create a new way of accumulating capital" (2017: 27). The rise of digital capitalism in the COVID-19 era can therefore be understood in the very context that is described by Srnicek. In this context, "digital capitalism" provides new remedies to revitalize the capitalist system to maintain economic growth in service of capitalist profits and at the expense of the working class. Whilst the COVID-19 pandemic has amplified the digital transformation of the economy, however, some businesses prove unable to compete, and certain skills are now out of demand as they are replaced by smart systems (Chou 2018).

An important consequence of the digital restructuring of the capitalist economy in response to the pandemic-related crisis is the consolidation of what came to be known as Big Tech, i.e., digital monopolies. Big Tech does not only provide a significant part of the technological infrastructure but also collects, owns, and manages data, including personal data, which gives it the power to heavily influence the global economic and geopolitical agenda of 21st-century capitalism. Big Tech can be treated as a technology oligarchy with immense wealth, influence, and power, dominating global trade and investment. The major Big Tech actors, Google-parent Alphabet, Apple, Amazon, and Microsoft have all reached the value of $1 trillion each, even though "Apple, Microsoft and Amazon … [have] slipped back to about $930 billion [by the beginning of 2020]. Adding Facebook into that group, the five most valuable U.S. tech companies are now worth a staggering $5.2 trillion…. That's up from 11% five years ago, with about two-thirds of the value, or $3.5 trillion, accruing over that stretch" (Levy 2020: para. 2–3). Their wealth immensely increased in the year 2020, as the pandemic brought new momentum to digitalization, and the top seven technology companies have added $3.4 trillion in value. Facebook, Tesla and Nvidia have joined the ranks of the aforementioned four companies (Levy 2020). Similarly, in the Chinese tech industry, Alibaba, Baidu, Huawei, JD.com, and Tencent are also among the companies that have gained immense worth (Watson 2020: 40). The monopolization by these companies and their massive gains led to a 16-month investigation by the Democratic members of the House Judiciary Subcommittee on Antitrust in the US, who presented an over 400-page antitrust report by the end of 2020, scrutinizing them for their massive market power and discussing what can be done to regulate the market. While the report includes various examples of how these companies have engaged in strategies that prevent innovation and reduce competition, the common allegation was that they acted as the gatekeepers of digital industries (Ghaffary and Del Rey 2020).

As part of the Big Tech business model, platformization can be seen as a key dynamic of digital capitalism, which consolidates the monopolizing tendencies of digital technology companies and intensifies data extraction and the commodification of data. Srnicek (2017) argues that the old business models were not fully suitable for maximizing profits extracted from data, which calls for a new type of firm: the platform. In his landmark book,

Platform Capitalism, Srnicek (2017) describes the platform fundamentally as the ideal way "to monopolise, extract, analyse, and use the increasingly large amounts of data that were being recorded" (29). Platforms provide the "digital infrastructures that enable two or more groups to interact [and t]hey, therefore, position themselves as intermediaries that bring together different users: customers, advertisers, service providers, producers, suppliers, and even physical objects" (30). They can gather data from a wide range of processes such as weather conditions, production processes and the behaviour of other organizational and individual users (30–32).

The platform model has a few advantages for digital capitalism. First, the platforms allow "their users to build their own products, services, and marketplaces" by providing the necessary infrastructure (Srnicek 2017: 30). This adaptable design, which is built on pre-existing infrastructure and cheap marginal costs for innovation, creates a space for the invention of endless new uses of platform capabilities, maintaining a constant source of profit for the platform owner. As different groups can mediate, the platform provides an advantage over traditional models since it offers access to, and can record, the data of digital interactions taking place between users in continuously increasing ways. For example, while Google records data on search activity, Facebook records data on social interactions between friends and family. Second, platforms rely on what Srnicek (2017) calls the "network effects" where the more people use the platform, the more valuable it becomes. The more users a platform attracts the better its algorithms, which make the platforms more useful. In turn, this makes the platform attract more users. This effect thus creates a tendency towards monopolization and "lends platforms a dynamic of ever-increasing access to more activities, and therefore to more data" (30). Third, the network effect enables the platforms to make use of "cross-subsidisation," where "one arm of the firm reduces the price of a service or good (even providing it for free), but another arm raises prices to make up for these losses" (31). This tactic can be used to attract more and more users to the platform through fine-tuning. Finally, while platforms appear to have no restrictions in terms of how users can utilize the platform, they indeed have their rules about interactions, services, and products, set by the platform owner, which are imposed in line with business goals and interests (31). Through the platform model, digital monopolies exercise massive control over data and how they are extracted, utilized, and sold.

The command of data essentially implies expansive surveillance of user behaviour in digital spaces. Our dependence on the internet, essentially for social participation, situates us at the centre of a capitalist surveillance project, making us vulnerable to the invasions of capital, pushing us to find justifications for our situation or to make a choice between bowing down to these practices or not being connected at all, if that is even possible (Zuboff 2019). We, as both individual and social actors, represent the very sources, of these data, where information about our navigation of the digital world is delivered through the platforms for free. Indeed, digital monopolies design and control this process to maximize their profits. This means that they essentially claim ownership over our feelings, ideas, preferences, voices, personalities, and relationships (Pringle 2020). Shoshana Zuboff (2019), in her groundbreaking book *The Age of Surveillance Capitalism*, calls this system "surveillance capitalism," where capital extracts data from every kind of human experience imaginable, through surveillance on our behaviour in the digital world:

> Surveillance capitalism unilaterally claims human experience as free raw material for translation into behavioral data. Although some of these data are applied to product or service improvement, the rest are declared as a proprietary behavioral surplus, fed into advanced manufacturing processes known as "machine intelligence," and fabricated into prediction products that anticipate what you will do now, soon, and later. Finally, these prediction products are traded in a new kind of marketplace for behavioral predictions that I call behavioral futures markets. Surveillance capitalists have grown immensely wealthy from these trading operations, for many companies are eager to lay bets on our future behavior. (14)

While the existence of surveillance capitalism cannot be imagined outside the digital world, Zuboff (2019) underlines that it is not the same thing as digital technology. She argues that how technological advancements are utilized, to what ends, for which goals, and by which rules depend on the social and economic logic behind it. Thus, it is the principles of the capitalist system that shapes how these technologies are used today, in ways that would try to take away human freedom and agency. However, surveillance capitalism as a strategic dimension of contemporary capitalism persuades us to think that their practices are inevitable manifestations of the technologies used, rather than "meticulously calculated and lavishly funded means to self-dealing commercial ends" (21). Moreover, extensive surveillance and invasive access to personal data also benefit political authorities and their state intelligence agencies. As the lack of effective laws about access to data gives surveillance capitalism massive opportunities to expand its projects, state agencies can benefit from this surveillance in maintaining the status-quo (Zuboff 2019).

Zuboff (2019) likens surveillance capitalism's feeding on each and every sphere of human experience to Karl Marx's image of capitalism as a vampire feeding on labour. As such, she describes Google, followed by other elements of the infamous GAFA (Amazon, Facebook, and Apple), as well as Microsoft, as the pioneer of surveillance capitalism, like Ford was the pioneer of managerial capitalism. She goes on to add that this business model is not exclusive to such companies and has now expanded to other internet-based businesses. In this process, as data are collected, Zuboff (2019) argues, individuals are persuaded through global technology to give up their privacy and to believe that they are "users," who will receive better products and improved service as a result. Quite conveniently, "Google's ex-CEO Eric Schmidt famously stated, 'If you have something that you don't want anyone to know, maybe you shouldn't be doing it in the first place.' Facebook boss Zuckerberg has argued the age of privacy is over" (Pringle 2020: para. 19). Based on such observations, Zuboff (2019) states that "we are the sources of surveillance capitalism's crucial surplus: the objects of a technologically advanced and increasingly inescapable raw-material-extraction operation. Surveillance capitalism's actual customers are the enterprises that trade in its markets for future behavior" (17). The algorithms of platforms are developed based on commercial ends since they are "inherently biased towards the advertisers and away from the needs of the consumers" (Brin and Page 1998). Through data mining, where raw data are turned into usable information in line with the goals of these businesses, users are tracked in various ways to learn and eventually predict and manipulate their behaviour. "Among the most frequently used techniques are 'cookies' or other relatively durable markers that are placed on the visitor's hard drive. These cookies make it possible for firms, or their representatives, to 'track' individuals as they move to different sites around the web. As testimony revealed to the [Federal Trade Commision], data gathered from this 'clickstream' is often combined with additional information acquired from third-party sources" (Gandy Jr. 2006: 366). This information is thus used to form a detailed consumer profile, including tastes, purchasing habits, and what the consumer considers necessary. Such predictions thus enable advertising companies' digital tools to make quick decisions on how ads can be delivered tailor-made to each consumer (Gandy Jr. 2006). Similarly, they allow digital companies to interpret queries based on guessing the most probable user intent. Even the auto corrections of queries, which are offered under the pretext of developing user experience, can manipulate the searches to make them fit in the most popular, commercial interpretations. Moreover, search engines are inclined to personalize the search results according to each individual's interpreted interests to provide them with customized products (Simpson 2012). This claim to "personalization" helps to hide the aggressive extraction of the most intimate parts of our lives by surveillance capitalism (Zuboff 2019).

Furthermore, Zuboff (2019) argues that "surveillance capitalists discovered that the most-predictive behavioral data come from intervening in the state of play in order to nudge, coax, tune, and herd behavior toward profitable outcomes" (15). Therefore, human experience data is also used to influence and modify our behaviour. By using "means of behavioral modification" capitalism today attempts to automate society through what Zuboff (2019) calls "instrumentarian power." "Instrumentarian power knows and shapes human behavior toward others' ends.… It works its will through the automated medium of an increasingly ubiquitous computational architecture of 'smart' networked devices, things, and spaces" (15). This power thus supports the intensification of the means of behavioural modification, increasingly influencing us to behave in certain ways in line with the interests of capital. For instance, "'all advertising changes our behaviour. It creates a demand for something, which in turn incites you to buy something. And it might do that in ways that we don't even notice.'" (Shaw, quoted in Pringle 2020: para. 25).

The corporate manipulation of behaviour is not limited to creating demand for certain products. It also includes a process of influencing our thoughts and opinions through the unequal distribution of information. Zuboff (2019) warns us about the unknowability of the design and algorithms of platform operations to the people, while surveillance capitalism owns and manages an unimaginable amount of information. This, Zuboff argues, creates asymmetries in the distribution of knowledge and power in the service of corporate interests, rather than our own. For instance, the internet is dominated by a handful of search engines, especially by one giant monopoly, Google. These engines' priority is not to democratize information for philanthropic reasons but to instrumentalize information mainly for practical purposes related to market interests (Mager 2012). This can be seen in the formation of "echo chambers." The "network effects" improve platform algorithms, which both attract more users by making the platform more useful and help it offer better individualized products and services. Thus, the creation of echo chambers, where individuals are clustered with like-minded others and are exposed to information parallel to their opinions, preferences, and tastes, benefits the platform. However, this also means that (digital and) surveillance capitalism can manipulate information and work its algorithms in creating different truths for the users. While "the proliferation of online echo chambers may be an inevitable outcome of basic cognitive and social processes facilitated by social media: namely, the human tendency to be influenced by information and opinions to which one is exposed, and that of disliking disagreeable social ties" (Sasahara et al. 2019: 14), we already know that social media platforms, Facebook and Twitter to name two, "use centralized algorithms among other processes that curate a user experience that would conform to the comfort zone of said user" (Muhammad 2020: para. 3).

Furthermore, the corporate inclination towards the construction of echo chambers contributes to the proliferation of misinformation. First of all, as echo chambers expose users to beliefs that are consistent with theirs and limit the exposure to the ones that challenge them, they gain the potential to reinforce false minority opinions, such as fabricated news, even when there is evidence against them. Second, echo chambers reinforce herding, "which may lead to quick and premature convergence to suboptimal solutions of complex problems and simplistic interpretations of complex issues" (Sasahara et al. 2019: 15). Third, as users are less exposed to diverse opinions, they are more likely to perceive content as new. Therefore, when false news is presented as novel, it leads to a more expansive consumption of misinformation (Sasahara et al. 2019).

The companies, in their command of the platform space, can also censor contents and impose direct control on what can be shared by the users. They can thus make decisions with political consequences regarding significant issues, such as gender equality and freedom of expression (Deutsche Welle 2021). For instance, Facebook has been scrutinized for years over the application of its "community standards," where it was protested over its censorship of female nipples, with no ban on male ones (Paul 2019). It even implemented AI technology that "cleans" the space automatically, without any human complaints. However, so far, it seems that it is far from being an ideal solution. "As Guardian Australia reported ... a user was suspended for posting an 1890s image of Aboriginal men in chains in response to the Australian prime minister's claim — on which he subsequently backtracked — that Australia didn't have slavery. It was an AI error but for people attempting to share the image or stories it seemed as though Facebook was taking an incorrect, hardline position on a particular issue while allowing other posts — including the US President Donald Trump's inflammatory posts — to remain untouched" (Taylor 2020: para. 5–8).

In another infamous example during the COVID-19 pandemic, Twitter banned former US President Donald Trump's account following the insurrection of his supporters against the presidential election results. Twitter has officially stated: "After close review of recent Tweets from the @realDonaldTrump account and the context around them — specifically how they are being received and interpreted on and off Twitter — we have permanently suspended the account due to the risk of further incitement of violence" (Twitter Inc. 2021: para. 1). In its report about the evaluation of this decision, Twitter stated that while their public interest framework, "exists to enable the public to hear from elected officials and world leaders directly," Trump's account violated their rules (Twitter Inc. 2021: para. 2). These examples of the criticisms of platform command can be easily multiplied (Suciu 2021). What is evident in such examples is that the platforms are taking political decisions with serious consequences, in each and every sphere of data and surveillance management, including the formation of community guidelines, implementation of these rules through human evaluations or AI technology, and administrative decisions about what is appropriate and acceptable.

Additionally, the surveillance we are subjected to is not limited to our online presence. Our physical behaviour is being watched through digital technologies led by corporate (and state) actors, which is intensified with expansive uses of cyber-physical systems during the COVID-19 pandemic. In our everyday routines, we are faced with a world where the IoT would not only monitor but predict our needs through devices such as Alexa and Google Assistant in our homes, maintaining constant connectivity with the owner companies, and giving them access to our most private surroundings (Chou 2018). Our use of, especially mobile, tools like cell phones leaves our digital fingerprints, where a trail can be formed of our physical movement and interaction through the data we generate. For instance, in China, "in Zhengzhou, police can ... create virtual alarms for when a person approaches a particular location. They can get updates on people every hour or every day. They can monitor whom those people have met with, especially if both people are on a blacklist for some kind of infraction, from committing a crime to skipping a debt payment" (Mozur and Krolik 2019: para. 22).

This extraction, control, and manipulation of data in exchange for our privacy and autonomy have serious implications for democracy. Zuboff (2019) warns us that "surveillance capitalism is a rogue force driven by novel economic imperatives that disregard social norms and nullify the elemental rights associated with individual autonomy that are essential to the very possibility of a democratic society" (18). In this sense, surveillance capitalism presents a break from earlier forms of capitalism in terms of the reach of unprecedented instrumentarian power, where it seeks to dominate all human, social, and political spaces, transforming "the market into a project of total certainty" (26). Thus, she describes surveillance capitalism as a coup from above, which undermines people's sovereignty. Here, "instrumentarian society is imagined as a human simulation of machine learning systems: a confluent hive mind in which each element learns and operates in concert with every other element. In the model of machine confluence, the 'freedom' of each individual machine is subordinated to the knowledge of the system as a whole. Instrumentarian power aims to organize, herd, and tune society to achieve a similar *social confluence,* in which group pressure and computational certainty replace politics and democracy, extinguishing the felt reality and social function of an individualized existence" (26). Zuboff argues that this system challenges two elemental rights of the people, our *right to the future tense* and *the right to sanctuary.* Under the first, it takes away our ability to imagine, aim and create a future, which she describes as an essential principle of our free will. With the second, it takes away our ability to seek refuge as it expands to all spaces of life and creates a world without exit.

In the final analysis, one could argue that surveillance capitalism — taken here as a manifestation of digital capitalism itself — has instrumentalized digital technologies based on a false claim to empower the individual and liberate people from the iron cage of bureaucracy. In practice, however, this capitalism reduces the society to a mathematical model, which is continuously monitored and engineered through digital technologies for profit maximization. In this way, human beings are abstracted from agency, human actions are automated, and collective memory is closely supervised.

Indeed, a global crisis like the COVID-19 pandemic does nothing but catalyze this transformation, which will be more thoroughly addressed in the next chapter. As social isolation and quarantine measures are implemented as among the most effective solutions to the pandemic, it provides further justification for surveillance where data are used to control those who carry the virus, inspect public spaces for threats, and draw risk maps for certain areas. Furthermore, against the reality of a life-threatening illness, individuals are faced with greater motivation to give up their privacy for the protection that this surveillance offers. It is highly likely that this new scope of surveillance brought by the pandemic will not be temporary. At this point, it would be helpful to put Naomi Klein's landmark work on the shock doctrine and disaster capitalism in conversation with Zuboff's theory on surveillance capitalism for a better understanding of the COVID-19 context, as we suggest in our next chapter.

Review and Discussion

In this chapter, we discussed the recent transformations of global capitalism against the backdrop of 4IR, where new technological advancements are instrumentalized to maximize corporate profits and accumulating capital by reference to the commodification of data, rising hyperconnectivity, automation, and the integration of the world with physical and biological spheres. These developments — which give the capitalist system the opportunity to become more "efficient" and "flexible" — have brought to the forefront the digitalizing tendencies of contemporary capitalism with a stronger emphasis on surveillance and social control. In the COVID-19 context, particularly, the growing salience of digital capitalism can be observed in the increased consumption of digital products and services through "platformification" as the "ideal" business model for the extraction and utilization of data. After reviewing how the proponents of digital capitalism celebrate these developments, we turned our attention to the societal costs of digital capitalism. Our critical analysis led us to reveal how Big Tech accumulates immense power and wealth, only to be accelerated under pandemic conditions. An important implication of digital capitalism led by Big Tech is the rise of surveillance capitalism as an extreme manifestation of digital capitalism that characterizes one of the most salient dimensions of the contemporary capitalist system. This is embodied in the instrumentarian power of capitalism, which inclines to create a system of total command and manipulation of human experience. Eventually, the COVID-19 period has exposed these instrumentarian inclinations that pose a foundational threat to democracy in all its forms. In the next chapter, we provide an in-depth analysis of how digital and surveillance capitalism instrumentalizes the COVID-19 crisis itself to advance this instrumentarian agenda even further.

REFERENCES

BDO. 2020. "COVID-19 Is Accelerating the Rise of the Digital Economy." *BDO*, May. <https://www.bdo.com/insights/business-financial-advisory/strategy,-technology-transformation/covid-19-is-accelerating-the-rise-of-the-digital-e>.

Brin, S., and L. Page. 1998. "The Anatomy of a Large-Scale Hypertextual Web Search Engine." <http://infolab.stanford.edu/~backrub/google.html>.

Caldwell, J.H., and D. Krishna. 2020. "The Acceleration of Digitization as a Result of COVID-19." *Deloitte*, July 30. <https://www2.deloitte.com/global/en/blog/responsible-business-blog/2020/acceleration-of-digitization-as-result-of-covid-19.html>.

Chandler, D., and C. Fuchs. 2019. "Introduction: Big Data Capitalism — Politics,

Activism, and Theory." In D. Chandler and C. Fuchs (eds.), *Digital Objects, Digital Subjects: Interdisciplinary Perspectives on Capitalism, Labour and Politics in the Age of Big Data.* (pp. 1–20). London: University of Westminster Press.

Chou, S. 2018. "The Fourth Industrial Revolution: Digital Fusion with Internet of Things." *Journal of International Affairs* 72, 1: 107–120.

Clément, T. 2015. "'Whistle While You Work': Work, Emotion, and Contests of Authority at the Happiest Place on Earth." In O. Fraysse and M. O'Neil (eds.), *Digital Labour and Prosumer Capitalism: The US Matrix* (pp. 145–165). Houndsmills: Palgrave Macmillan.

Deutsche Welle. 2021. "Angela Merkel Calls Trump Twitter Ban 'Problematic'." *Deutsche Welle,* January 11. <https://www.dw.com/en/angela-merkel-calls-trump-twitter-ban-problematic/a-56197684>.

Fuchs, C. 2015. *Culture and Economy in the Age of Social Media.* New York: Routledge.

Gandy Jr., O. 2006. "Data Mining, Surveillance, and Discrimination in the Post-9/11 Environment." In R.V. Ericson and K.D. Haggerty (eds.), *The New Politics of Surveillance and Visibility* (pp. 363–384). Toronto: University of Toronto Press.

Ghaffary, S., and J. Del Rey. 2020. "The Big Tech Antitrust Report Has One Big Conclusion: Amazon, Apple, Facebook, and Google Are Anti-Competitive." *Vox,* October 6. <https://www.vox.com/recode/2020/10/6/21505027/congress-big-tech-antitrust-report-facebook-google-amazon-apple-mark-zuckerberg-jeff-bezos-tim-cook>.

Heller, H. 2011. *The Birth of Capitalism: A 21st Century Perspective.* London: Pluto Press.

Kobrin, S.J. 1998. "Back to the Future: Neomedievalism and the Postmodern Digital World Economy." *Journal of International Affairs* 51, 2: 361–386.

LaBerge, L., C. O'Toole, J. Schneider, and K. Smaje. 2020. "How COVID-19 Has Pushed Companies Over the Technology Tipping Point—and Transformed Business Forever." *McKinsey&Company.* October 5. <https://www.mckinsey.com/business-functions/strategy-and-corporate-finance/our-insights/how-covid-19-has-pushed-companies-over-the-technology-tipping-point-and-transformed-business-forever>.

Leatherby, L., and D. Gelles. 2020. "How the Virus Transformed the Way Americans Spend Their Money." *The New York Times,* April 11. <https://www.nytimes.com/interactive/2020/04/11/business/economy/coronavirus-us-economy-spending.html>.

Levy, A. 2020. "Big Tech Is Worth Over $5 Trillion Now That Alphabet Has Joined the Four Comma Club." *CNBC,* January 16. <https://www.cnbc.com/2020/01/16/big-tech-worth-over-5-trillion-with-alphabet-joining-four-comma-club.html>.

Mager, A. 2012. "Algorithmic Ideology." *Information, Communication & Society* 15, 5: 769–787.

Maheshwari, S., and M. Corkery. 2020. "U.S. Retail Crisis Deepens as Hundreds of Thousands Lose Work." *The New York Times,* March 30. <https://www.nytimes.com/2020/03/30/business/coronavirus-retail-furloughs-macys.html>.

Mozur, P., and A. Krolik. 2019. "A Surveillance Net Blankets China's Cities, Giving Police Vast Powers." *The New York Times,* December 17. <https://www.nytimes.

com/2019/12/17/technology/china-surveillance.html>.

Muhammad, Z. 2020. "Study Reveals How Social Media Algorithms Create Echo Chambers." *Digital Information World*, June 13. <https://www. digitalinformationworld.com/2020/06/study-reveals-how-social-media-algorithms-create-echo-chambers.html>.

Ollman, B. 1971. *Alienation: Marx's Conception of Man in a Capitalist Society.* Cambridge: Cambridge University Press.

Paul, K. 2019. "Naked Protesters Condemn Nipple Censorship at Facebook Headquarters." *The Guardian*, June 3. <https://www.theguardian.com/technology/2019/jun/03/facebook-nude-nipple-protest-wethenipple>.

Philbeck, T., and N. Davis. 2018. "The Fourth Industrial Revolution: Shaping a New Era." *Journal of International Affairs* 72, 1: 17–22.

Pollitzer, E. 2018. "Creating a Better Future: Four Scenarios for How Digital Technologies Could Change the World." *Journal of International Affairs* 72, 1: 75–90.

Pozdnyakova, U.A., V.V. Golikov, I.A. Peters, and I.A. Morozova. 2019. "Genesis of the Revolutionary Transition to Industry 4.0 in the 21st Century and Overview of Previous Industrial Revolutions." In E.G. Popkova, Y.V. Ragulina, and A.V. Bogoviz (eds.), *Industry 4.0: Industrial Revolution of the 21st Century* (pp. 11–19). Cham: Springer.

Pringle, R. 2020. "Surveillance Capitalism: Who Is Watching Us Online — And Why?" CBC, November 10. <https://www.cbc.ca/radio/ideas/surveillance-capitalism-who-is-watching-us-online-and-why-1.5791546>.

PwC. 2020. "Going Digital During COVID-19 and Beyond." <https://www.pwccn.com/en/tmt/going-digital-during-covid-19-beyond-jul2020.pdf>.

Sasahara, K., et al. 2019. "On the Inevitability of Online Echo Chambers." May 10. <https://arxiv.org/pdf/1905.03919v1.pdf>.

Schwab, K. 2016. *The Fourth Industrial Revolution*. Geneva: World Economic Forum.

Simpson, T.W. 2012. "Evaluating Google as an Epistemic Tool." *Metaphilosophy* 43, 4: 426–445.

Srnicek, N. 2017. *Platform Capitalism*. Cambridge: Polity Press.

Suciu, P. 2021. "Do Social Media Companies Have the Right to Silence the Masses — And Is This Censoring the Government?" *Forbes*, January 11. <https://www.forbes.com/sites/petersuciu/2021/01/11/do-social-media-companies-have-the-right-to-silence-the-masses--and-is-this-censoring-the-government/?sh=24cdfcc48e2d>.

Tan, T., and W. Shang-Su. 2017. "Public Policy Implications of the Fourth Industrial Revolution for Singapore." *S. Rajaratnam School of International Studies*. October. <https://www.rsis.edu.sg/wp-content/uploads/2017/12/PR171220_Public-Policy-Implications-of-the-Fourth-Industrial-Revolution-for-Singapore_WEB.pdf>.

Taylor, J. 2020. "Not Just Nipples: How Facebook's AI Struggles to Detect Misinformation." *The Guardian*, June 16. <https://www.theguardian.com/technology/2020/jun/17/not-just-nipples-how-facebooks-ai-struggles-to-detect-misinformation>.

Twitter Inc. 2021. "Permanent Suspension of @realDonaldTrump." Twitter

Inc, January 8. <https://blog.twitter.com/en_us/topics/company/2020/
suspension.html>.

Wajcman, J. 2015. *Pressed for Time: The Acceleration of Life in Digital Capitalism.*
Chicago: University of Chicago Press.

Watson, V.B. 2020. "The Fourth Industrial Revolution and Its Discontents:
Governance, Big Tech, and the Digitization of Geopolitics." In A.L. Vuving
(ed.), *Hindsight, Insight, Foresight: Thinking About Security in the Indo-Pacific* (pp.
37–48). Honolulu: Daniel K. Inouye Asia-Pacific Center for Security Studies.

Zuboff, S. 2019. *The Age of Surveillance Capitalism: The Fight for a Human Future at the
New Frontier of Power.* London: Profile Books.

2 From Digital and Surveillance to Disaster Capitalism

How Organized Fear Catalyzes a New Global Political Economy

I n the previous chapter, we addressed the contemporary transformations of global capitalism where the digital and surveillance-related aspects of capitalism take increasing precedence. With this chapter, we shift our focus to how capitalism helps to catalyze the rise of digital and surveillance capitalism in the COVID-19 era. Against this backdrop, the present chapter builds on a comparative reading of the "disaster capitalism" approach and the study of "cultures of fear" to provide a systematic explanation of how the agenda of digital and surveillance capitalism is accelerated. We argue that the cultivation and diffusion of a culture of fear erected on world-historical disastrous events serve as an important medium for the current transformation of global capitalism. In this context, we draw on the ways in which neoliberalism was globally instituted as the organizing principle of the US-led world order in a political-economic and cultural context constructed around disasters. The focus is on emblematic cases that illustrate the symbiotic relationship between neoliberalism and the culture of fear as a constitutive element of the US-centred world order: the Pinochet coup in Chile and Argentina's military dictatorship era, "shock therapy" economics in Russia, and the US war on terror following 9/11. Our inferences from these cases are used to perform an anticipatory analysis of how the COVID-19 pandemic may give way to a world-historical transformation based on a rapidly spreading culture of fear.

Our chapter is structured as follows. The first section conceptually explains the symbiotic relationship between disaster capitalism, neoliberalism, and the culture of fear. The second is devoted to case studies that showcase this relationship. In the third section, we recontextualize our study within the framework of the COVID-19 pandemic. Our chapter closes with a section that revisits surveillance capitalism in its relationship to Big Tech and disasters.

Disaster Capitalism and the Culture of Fear

The term "disaster capitalism" was coined by Naomi Klein (2007), who based her conceptual framework on the critique of neoliberalism. In her lexicon, neoliberalism refers to a policy paradigm defined by three landmark demands: privatization, government deregulation, and deep cuts to social spending. Her polemic against neoliberalism focuses especially on Milton Friedman, one of the most prominent neoliberal thinkers. Reflecting on Hurricane Katrina — among the most devastating natural disasters in US history — Milton Friedman recommended the US government to dismantle its public education system by extending the network of charter schools and distributing vouchers to households for food access. Ultimately, Klein shows that the Katrina disaster provided an opportunity for the Bush administration to implement Friedman's neoliberal recommendations (Klein 2007). Based on similar cases, Klein advances the argument that global capitalism instrumentalizes human-caused or natural disasters (e.g., military coups, terrorist incidents, economic crises, wars, earthquakes, tsunamis, hurricanes) for the sake of advancing its own agenda of renewal and reconstruction. According to her, such disorienting disasters help to suspend public debate and suppress democratic practices. This allows capitalists to exploit the window of opportunity opened by traumatic shocks (Klein 2007).

Undoubtedly, capitalism cannot succeed in rejuvenating itself merely through top-down policy impositions. It needs to secure popular consent from the ground up. In this regard, we believe that the study of "cultures of fear" is helpful for a deeper understanding of the inner mechanism of disaster capitalism. A culture of fear is a system of beliefs, values, and behavioural patterns rooted in negative emotions such as fear and terror, which can be used as "affective tools of government that come into being as a modus of population management deployed by military, political, and administrative actors" (Linke and Smith 2009: 5). It feeds off a strong sense of existential insecurity that inflates the meaning of harm and fosters a mood of mistrust. This is facilitated by simplistic blaming of the media and the propagation of alarmist reactions meshed with catastrophic rhetoric (Furedi 2018). In certain cases, the end result is the formation and consolidation of an imagined community united against the threat of the Other, whoever or whatever that might be. In this way, global capitalism can easily deploy a securocratic language around disastrous events to emotionally mobilize popular support and execute its own programmatic agenda conducive to large-scale transformations in the world order (Linke and Smith 2009). e.g., an environmentally responsible digital (and surveillance) capitalism in the case of COVID-19. Ultimately, fear becomes "a central figure of global social life" (Linke and Smith 2009: 4).

Neoliberalism and Disaster Capitalism in Action: A Historical Perspective

Chile is widely regarded as the first laboratory of neoliberalism: the later structural adjustment programs of the International Monetary Fund (IMF) and the World Bank were modelled on the Chilean experiment. In fact, the case of Chile perfectly reveals how the roots of neoliberalism formed in world-historical disasters are constitutive of the US-centred world order. Chile's socialist president Salvador Allende was overthrown in 1973 by a military coup led by Augusto Pinochet and actively supported by the United States. In 1975, Chile transitioned to neoliberal capitalism under the guidance of the Chicago Boys: neoliberal economic advisors, most of whom were trained at prominent American institutions such as at the University of Chicago, Harvard University, and the Massachusetts Institute of Technology (Klein 2007). Chile's neoliberal restructuring owed its power to widescale social pacification: the military junta cracked down on opposition forces and inculcated a culture of fear, ensuring compliance with neoliberal shock therapy measures. Estimates suggest that in the Pinochet era, more than 3,000 people disappeared and tens of thousands were jailed, tortured, and/or exiled. This repressive environment strengthened Pinochet's hand in reducing import tariffs and social expenditure, abolishing price controls, carrying out mass privatization, and debilitating unions. Ultimately, Pinochet's shock therapy exposed Chile to deep recessions in 1975 and 1982 and contributed to extreme levels of inequality. Chile's Gini coefficient rose from around 0.45 in the mid-1970s to over 0.6 by the end of the 1980s (Taylor 2006). Moreover, the replication of the Chilean model in the rest of the region resulted in disaster. The number of people in poverty in Latin America grew from 118 million in 1980 to 196 million in 1990. The region's total foreign debt increased from US$31.3 billion in 1972 to US$430 billion in the late 1980s, and US$750 billion by the 2000s. In the period 1981–2000, average annual economic growth was only 1.6% in Argentina, 2.1% in Brazil, and 2.7% in Mexico (Saad Filho, Iannini, and Molinari 2007).

The mobilization of fear through military coups was also instrumental in the case of Argentina's transition to neoliberalism under US influence. Argentina stepped into a long era of military dictatorship when Isabel Perón's government was overthrown by General Jorge Rafael Videl as part of Operation Condor, a US-backed campaign of state and paramilitary terror in support of right-wing dictatorships in Latin America. This period — also called the Dirty War era (1976–83) — led to the disappearance of 30,000 people, along with other human rights violations including child kidnappings (Hellinger 2014).

This environment of public fear was used by the military junta to impose neoliberal restructuring on the Argentine economy (Klein 2007). In 1976, thanks to US support for the military dictatorship, Argentina was granted "the largest loan ever to a Latin American country" (Cooney 2007). In line with the newly adopted neoliberal agenda, the country initiated a radical deindustrialization policy that accentuated agroindustry in favour of the landed oligarchy. This process went hand in hand with financial deregulation and the suppression of unions. Argentina witnessed a record increase in foreign debt, from US$9.7 billion in 1976 to over US$45 billion in 1983 (Cooney 2007).

A world-historical disaster of an even greater magnitude took place in Boris Yeltsin's Russia in 1991–99, following the collapse of the Soviet Union. Yeltsin took advantage of the environment of fear and confusion created by the disintegration of the Soviet Union to launch a shock therapy campaign with the aim of liberalizing the Russian economy. The campaign started in 1992, with the IMF's active support: Yeltsin made a hasty move to liberalize prices and trade, which was followed by mass privatizations. An important side effect of these privatizations was the emergence of a new stratum of Russian oligarchs feeding off rising corruption in the Yeltsin era (Bedirhanoğlu 2004). The shock therapy resulted in average real pay falling by almost 50% in the period 1990–95. Organized crime grew to such an extent that up to 80% of private banks and businesses in major cities were involved with "mafia" organizations (Kotz and Weir 2007). In the long run, excessive liberalization and indebtedness exposed Russia to the negative effects of the 1997 Asian financial crisis. This eventually marked the end of the Yeltsin era and paved the way for Vladimir Putin's rise to power (Baiman, Boushey, and Dawn 2000: 210–217).

The post-9/11 conjuncture is an important example of how the world order is shaped by the symbiotic relationship between disaster capitalism and the neoliberal culture of fear (Mendieta 2011). On September 11, 2001, four passenger planes were hijacked by terrorists affiliated with al-Qaeda. Two of the planes crashed into the World Trade Center complex and the third into the Pentagon, while the fourth plane crashed in a field near Shanksville, Pennsylvania. The attacks claimed nearly 3,000 lives and resulted in more than 25,000 injuries. The collective trauma created by these attacks served as a historic opportunity for the United States to launch the "war on terror": a strategic campaign for restructuring the world order in pursuit of its imperialist agenda. As such, "the Bush administration outsourced, with no public debate, many of the most sensitive and core functions of government — from providing health care to soldiers, to interrogating prisoners, to gathering and 'data mining' information on all of us" (Klein 2007: 12). The enacting of the USA Patriot Act enabled the government to suppress civil liberties and enhance the influence of the US military- and prison-industrial complexes. Mass surveillance and incarceration thus became the norm (Klein 2007; Mendieta 2011). The driving agenda was not limited to reasserting the waning importance of US interventionism in the absence of the Soviet Union and reordering the Greater Middle East with the aim of inhibiting the rise of potential US rivals in Eurasia. The United States was also interested in refuelling its stagnating neoliberal economy based on a military stimulus. This was particularly seen in the US occupation of Afghanistan since 2001, the War on Iraq, and other interventions, for example in Libya and Syria as part of the so-called "Arab Spring."

In summary, these cases demonstrate how disastrous events such as terrorist attacks, state failures, and military coups lead to large-scale transformations that open up new possibilities for neoliberal restructuring on a global scale. Disaster-led crises sweep away the conditions for healthy public deliberation; this process is facilitated by an authoritarian environment of fear and confusion. Such an environment is easily exploited by capitalist interests in favour of an agenda of renewal and reconstruction. In particular, the post-9/11 conjuncture strongly exemplifies the ways in which disaster capitalism reproduces itself by deploying an Islamophobic culture of fear, where highly inflated and alarmist reactions help to reorganize the world order in line with the catastrophic rhetoric of the war on terror.

COVID-19 and the Collective Mobilization of Fear

The above cases can give us valuable insights into the possible ways in which the covid-19 pandemic may pave the way for a paradigm shift in the world order. Worthy of mention in this regard is Giorgio Agamben's thesis of a "state of exception." In the early days of the covid-19 pandemic, Italian philosopher Agamben asserted that the danger of the disease was highly exaggerated. According to him, the pandemic is a socially constructed phenomenon, which helps governments to create a state of exception in deploying extraordinary measures that might have been difficult to implement under normal circumstances. In other words, Agamben claimed that governments purposefully exaggerated the risks of the pandemic in order to implement new social control devices and methods (Agamben 2020). Though he may have underestimated the lethal potential of the pandemic, there seems to be some value in taking his "state of exception" thesis seriously. The pandemic of COVID-19 has great potential to be used by capitalist forces to reinvent the capitalist system or postpone the collapse of global capitalism by exploiting widespread anxiety and panic. By creating a culture of fear that feeds off the COVID-19 disaster, global capitalism can potentially incapacitate anti-systemic forces through increased use of new surveillance technologies and enhanced social-distancing strategies.

It is known that infectious diseases can trigger negative psychological effects such as hypochondriasis and anxiety (Duncan, Schaller, and Park 2009). The COVID-19 pandemic is no exception to this psychological peril. A case in point is a survey by Wang and his team, which reveals the psychological damage that the pandemic caused in China during its early phases. In this study, 16.5% of respondents showed moderate to severe depression symptoms while 28.8% of them experienced anxiety problems and 8.1% had high stress levels (Wang et al. 2020). Similarly, in a survey conducted during the lockdown period in Italy, 17.3% of respondents said they had depression while 20.8% admitted having anxiety problems (Rossi et al. 2020). In a similar vein, the COVID-19 pandemic has exposed the people of Italy to intense stress, closely associated with high levels of uncertainty as to how long it will take for Italy to return to normal and whether the pandemic will affect loved ones (Montemurro 2020). The COVID-19 pandemic may really have engendered a collective trauma and mass anxiety that can be easily taken advantage of by global capitalism.

Another important observer who anticipates the potentially dangerous outcomes of the COVID-19 pandemic is Slavoj Žižek. He claims that there is no turning back to normal and that this pandemic will irreversibly change our lives. Žižek implies that the pandemic will have paradigm-shifting effects for the world. In his opinion, the pandemic can only have two possible outcomes: either a new normal will be constructed "on the ruins of our old lives" or a new form of barbarism will emerge (Žižek 2020: 3). Žižek goes on to suggest that the pandemic has the potential to engender the worst socioeconomic catastrophe since the Great Depression. In this new period, markets will not be able to prevent the forthcoming waves of poverty and chaos. Moreover, Žižek does not believe that developing medical treatments or a vaccine will suffice to reverse the crisis of global capitalism (Žižek 2020). Indeed, even when the pandemic is brought under control, the markets may not function as they used to, because the risk of a new wave of COVID-19 could discourage investments and lead to monopolistic prices at the expense of lower income groups.

Žižek maintains that the pandemic can only be controlled by using a different paradigm to neoliberalism; that is, through large-scale measures including government-imposed quarantines. Furthermore, he points to the fact that the spontaneous functioning of markets would eventually deepen the inequalities and hamper access to basic necessities and services. As such, the risk of economic disaster can only be averted through globally coordinated efforts; not only in the battle against the disease, but also in production and distribution. In the meantime, Žižek expresses optimism that this crisis presents a universal threat and therefore may give birth to global solidarity inasmuch as it invites us to reconsider "the very basic features of the society." In this sense, the WHO's global coordination efforts at leading this process based on precise and scientific recommendations without causing panic can be seen as a key catalyst for an emergent solidarity on a global scale (Žižek 2020: 41). This is in contrast to US efforts to delegitimize the WHO by reference to its alleged "China-centric" approach (Deutsche Welle 2020a).

In contrast to the WHO's responsible approach, certain world leaders are not interested in following scientific guidance, preventing mass panic, or promoting global solidarity. Agamben (2020) underlines the fact that public authorities — and the mass media — contribute to the diffusion of panic at first hand. For instance, former US president Donald Trump did not restrain himself from amplifying popular anxiety with his statements highlighting the number of potential fatalities from COVID-19; at the very beginning of the pandemic, these were estimated at somewhere between 100,000 and 240,000 (Lovelace and Mangan 2020). Similarly, UK Prime Minister Boris Johnson has not hesitated to stir mass panic by warning his people to be prepared "to lose loved ones to coronavirus" (Hughes and Payne 2020). Yet political restraint could have played a key role in reducing pandemic-related social risks. One possible explanation for this situation is that leading politicians in Western societies are seeking to capitalize on a historical opportunity to reorganize global capitalism by justifying extraordinary measures through manufactured mass panic and Sinophobia. Therefore, they are mobilizing a culture of fear predicated on the COVID-19 disaster. As such, China's geopolitical isolation can be used to re-industrialize capitalism in core countries, reverse the increasing Chinese influence on global governance, and postpone the multipolarization of the world order.

Yuval Noah Harari's warnings buttress this possibility of exploiting the disaster for a fear-driven political agenda. A state of horror triggered by economic and social turbulence can encourage society as a whole to search for a strong leader who will restore public order. This is similar to how the incessant economic disasters in post–World War I Germany resulted in the rise of the Nazis to power. Harari thus underlines how a crisis can be a turning point for a society, or a decisive moment to determine the direction of history. The COVID-19 pandemic is exemplary of such a milestone. It marks one of the deepest crises in recent history, which will surely have serious ramifications, not only for public health but also for the global economy, world politics, and culture (Harari 2020). According to Harari, the human species will certainly survive the pandemic, but the world will be subjected to a deep-seated structural crisis. He goes on to argue that today's political choices will greatly affect how the post-coronavirus world takes shape.

Similar to how Agamben cautions about a disease-induced "state of exception," Harari refers to the "nature of emergencies," underlining how these are "fast-forward historical processes," and there are some "short-term emergency measures" that can be implemented to overcome the crisis (Harari 2020). We are already seeing the rapid proliferation of immature technologies such as distance-education platforms and teleworking environments. The diffusion of such technologies in the post-coronavirus era may result in the permanentizing of precarious labour practices (e.g., temporary employment, lower wages, de-unionization, job insecurity) and the intensification of labour exploitation (e.g., unpaid overtime and further disturbance of work-life balance). Meanwhile, governments across the world have already declared states of emergency and started to take extraordinary measures to counter the pandemic. One of these measures is the implementation of new surveillance technologies on the pretext of controlling the contagion. For instance, the UK government has adapted its facial recognition systems to identify COVID-19 victims (Tovey 2020). Another case in point is how Israeli Prime Minister Benjamin Netanyahu has authorized the use of surveillance technology, normally designed for anti-terrorist activities (Harari 2020). Coupled with the proliferation of mass anxiety, "social" isolation and new surveillance technologies, the perpetuation of authoritarian government practices may seriously undermine the mobilizing potential of popular movements against neoliberal capitalism and imperialism. These possibilities parallel Harari's observations: he suggests that the implementation of biological and emotional surveillance is another possible outcome. What is more, once these measures are normalized, they may become permanent, in the same way as the extraordinary antiterrorist measures adopted in the post-9/11 era (Harari 2020).

According to Harari, our political choices are important. Like Žižek, he believes that we need a global plan that avoids isolationism and encourages the free flow of information and equipment all over the globe, since the pandemic cannot be regionally contained. Moreover, global cooperation requires stronger trust in science and close care for personal hygiene, regular handwashing, and physical distancing. Just as Žižek advocates a stronger state to deal with the crisis, Harari maintains that the state's role is crucial in this period and surveillance is necessary to overcome the pandemic. However, he also cautions that data collected for this purpose should not be exploited to invent "an all-powerful government" (Harari 2020). According to Harari, more dangerous than the disease itself is "our own hatred, greed and ignorance," which may even set the stage for a new dictatorship under mass panic (Deutsche Welle 2020b).

In this sense, mass surveillance on social media platforms such as YouTube, WhatsApp, Twitter, and Facebook — as well as banning and removing content associated with "false" news and "conspiracy" — risk generating new forms of censorship to sustain the relations of domination and oppression. While Harari shares Žižek's optimism about the prospects for global cooperation, he also cautions that these prospects are threatened by a growing tendency towards scapegoating or targeting minorities and rival nations. Such tendencies — which are perhaps most strongly reflected in a Sinophobic culture of fear in Western nations — evoke the pre-World War II period during which protectionism increasingly gained currency and minorities such as Jews and Roma were persecuted. At this point, Žižek calls for caution about a possible return to the premodern state of reason after COVID-19 (Žižek 2020: 14). Even though developed countries benefit from higher educational standards, their citizens can be prone to anthropomorphizing the COVID-19 pandemic. The origins of this regression of reason may be found in mass anxiety and panic, which are further provoked by political authorities and corporate media (Žižek 2020).

According to Žižek, rational thinking dictates the necessity for collective struggle against the pandemic and stronger social policies geared towards protecting society as a whole. On any account, Žižek reasons that our health and welfare are inextricably linked to those of others, which brings forth the principle of altruism at the expense of absolute individualism.

However, in the case of COVID-19, Žižek's reasoning does not seem to fit the facts. Individualism may well be taking on increasing importance to the extent that people have started to see others, not only as potential rivals in the marketplace, but as "biological threats." Enhanced individualism also has the potential to atomize society by fostering anxiety, especially when individuals withdraw themselves into their own private domains and see the public domain as inherently threatening. Such perceptions can be easily manipulated by political authorities, such as Trump and Johnson, who are interested in taking advantage of disastrous situations. Put differently, a panic environment facilitated by public authorities may result in increased mass anxiety as a coping mechanism in the face of disastrous or threatening situations.

On the one hand, the COVID-19 pandemic may further exacerbate the global economic crisis, with the total disappearance of growth, a ubiquitous rise in unemployment and debts, and a cascade of bankruptcies across the world. On the other, it may have already started to create material conditions for the reproduction of neoliberal individualism. Perhaps most importantly, the meaning of self-quarantine against COVID-19 may be extended from mere home isolation to the normalization of self-interested behaviour. When society allows itself to be taken over by fear, individuals become more prone to pursuing nothing else but their own well-being and daily survival. In this environment, those in power positions could easily seize the moment to reshape the public domain in line with their agenda. This means that the COVID-19 pandemic may not be the absolute end of neoliberalism per se, even though it has exposed the deepening of the crisis of global capitalism. Under the influence of self-interested politicians, mass anxiety — as a popular self-defence mechanism against dangerous situations — risks the retreating of individuals, not only into their apartments but also into their narrow individual interests.

Revisiting Surveillance Capitalism in a World of Disasters: The Case of Big Tech

Based on our previous chapter in dialogue with Agamben and Harari's observations, one could argue that the COVID-19 pandemic has provided a perfect moment to expand the reach of surveillance capitalism. While the use of digital technologies is intensified during this period, thus providing more data than ever, the pandemic conditions supply the most desirable justifications for the expansion of instrumentarian power. Naomi Klein (2020) calls this moment "screen new deal," a pandemic shock doctrine, which is being fully implemented under the conditions of lockdown and social isolation. Klein (2020) argues that the COVID-19 pandemic has given the ideal opportunity to Big Tech to implement its corporate vision, where technology gets to be permanently integrated in our everyday lives, "a living laboratory for a permanent — and highly profitable — no-touch future" (para. 6). Under this doctrine, "humanlessness" and "contactlessness" are depicted as the ultimate advantages of technology since "humans are bio-hazards, machines are not" in the world of viruses (Klein 2020: para. 7).

Parallel to Zuboff's (2019) claim that we are giving up our right to sanctuary, Klein (2020) argues that this future we are being rushed into by the technology companies is one where we lose our exclusive access to personal spaces, in a "no exit" society. The most fundamental institutions of everyday life, our homes, schools, offices, and hospitals are and will be under further surveillance through constant connectivity. "It's a future in which our every move, our every word, our every relationship is trackable, traceable, and data-mineable by unprecedented collaborations between government and tech giants," with the infiltration of instrumentarian power in every corner of human experience (para. 9). Klein (2020), like Zuboff (2019), states that this future dependence on technology is marketed to us under the promise of convenience, frictionlessness, and personaliza-tion. While many people raised concerns regarding the human benefits of these technologies, regarding quality of life in relation to various social and political institutions, there were voices rising against the massive monetary gains and monopolization of Big Tech. However, these concerns are shut down with the panic that came with the COVID-19 pandemic, where this depiction of the future is being rebranded. As people are faced with a virus with no explicit cure and no ultimate protection, yet, these technologies are presented as the only ways "to pandemic-proof our lives, the indispens-able keys to keeping ourselves and our loved ones safe" (Klein 2020: para. 12). For instance, the voice recognition technology of Amazon's Alexa is highlighted as a marvelous solution to contexts that necessitate hand-free features, such as hospitals (Soper 2020). Its uses are praised for enabling quick communication during emergencies (Rubin 2020), from checking potential coronavirus symptoms to even providing a simulation of emotional contact in time of social isolation (Soper 2020). As Zuboff (2019) warned, the Big Tech companies once again are able to camouflage the capitalist logic behind using technological tools in intended ways and can present their existing and envisioned practices as not just inevitable consequences of technology, but also as ideal solutions to our needs when we are faced with such a crisis.

As we discussed in the previous chapter, Zuboff (2019) shows how the technology companies were already pushing this vision forward before the pandemic. In her turn, Klein (2020) draws attention to the relationship of these technology giants with governments around the world, once more, using the pandemic as the opportunity to expand their collaborations. In this sense, she shows how the project Zuboff (2019) calls "social confluence" is not only on its way but how the pandemic has accelerated its implementation. On the one hand, public voices and concerns about both the public resources allocated to these technologies and the implications of their implementation are pushed back. "Now, in the midst of the carnage of this ongoing pandemic, and the fear and uncertainty about the future it has brought, these companies clearly see their moment to sweep out all that democratic engagement," which they see as an inconvenience, an obstacle, in the full realization of their visions (Klein 2020: para. 38). On the other hand, there occurs a "seamless integration of government with a handful of Silicon Valley giants — with public schools, hospitals, doctor's offices, police, and military all outsourcing (at a high cost) many of their core functions to private tech companies" (Klein 2020: para. 15). The lobbying efforts by Big Tech have yielded fruitful results for companies in furthering their relationships with and influence on the government, manifested in former Google CEO Eric Schmidt's roles "as chair of the Defense Innovation Board, which advises the Department of Defense on increased use of artificial intelligence in the military, and as chair of the powerful National Security Commission on Artificial Intelligence, or NSCAI, which advises Congress on 'advances in artificial intelligence, related machine learning developments, and associated technologies,' with the goal of addressing 'the national and economic security needs of the United States, including economic risk'" (Klein 2020: para. 16). Among the board members of both organizations are executives from the members of Big Tech, including Microsoft, Amazon, and Facebook. Their main goal is to increase government spending on technology-enabling infrastructure and digital companies to obtain more power and autonomy, with the main reasoning that "public-private partnerships in mass surveillance and data collection" is a necessary measure to compete with China for world domination, which is supposedly inseparably linked to advances in technology and commercial power (Klein 2020: para. 21).

Indeed, the pandemic breathed new life to the lobbying efforts of Big Tech. The framing of requests involving public expenditure, "'public-private partnerships' in AI, and for the loosening of myriad privacy and safety protections" started to be presented as necessary measures for the protection of public health and essential workers (Klein 2020: para. 30). For instance, the crisis can be depicted as an opportunity to experiment with remote education and other strategic sectors such as health (Klein 2020: para. 35). Klein thus evaluates this moment as an opportunity for these corporations to dispense with democratic regulation, without the challenging voices of labour or civil rights, where they use the fear and the uncertainty brought by the pandemic to recognize "a utopia of certainty" (Zuboff 2019).

Indeed, there are numerous examples of how these companies collaborate with governments around the world to implement these technologies. Primarily, Chinese disease surveillance practices of their citizens are unmatched, with access to and monitoring of their social media apps, and an advanced facial recognition technology that can identify individuals even when they have their masks on, developed by China's leading company in recognition technology, Hanwang Technology Co. (Hanvon) (Roberts 2020). China has also used drones to enforce quarantines and citizens are required to scan QR codes that measure the risk of exposure to the virus, which is utilized for assigning permissions on entering public spaces (Roberts 2020; Whitehead 2020). In Singapore, Bluetooth technology is used to alert people about their physical contacts with those who carry the virus, through the TraceTogether app (Whitehead 2020), and in Taiwan, an "electric fence" program is implemented where quarantined persons' physical location is tracked through their mobile phones to ensure that they stay home (Roberts 2020). "The Australian government has contracted with Amazon to store the data for its controversial coronavirus tracking app. The Canadian government has contracted with Amazon to deliver medical equipment, raising questions about why it bypassed the public postal service" (Klein 2020: para. 39). Similarly, in the United Kingdom, the National Health Service announced that it collaborates with technology firms, including Google, Amazon and data-processing company Palantir, to implement a platform for disease surveillance (Roberts 2020). Moreover, the United States and Russia have showed interest in facial recognition technologies, like China, which "has long been seen as the endgame in the battle between personal freedom and digital surveillance (Whitehead 2020: para. 5).

Review and Discussion

The history of neoliberalism since the 1970s shows how global capitalism can shape the world order by instrumentalizing disastrous events. We observe that inculcating a culture of fear serves as a strategic means to legitimize paradigmatic policy shifts so as to radically alter the structure of the world order. Characteristic of such cultural practices is the deployment of a securocratic language around disaster, similar to the anti-communism of putschists in Latin America and the case of post 9/11 Islamophobia. Military, political, and administrative actors capitalize on heightening feelings of existential insecurity, panic, and anxiety resulting from disasters, such as the collapse of the Soviet Union. As such, they can encourage alarmist reactions and exploit people's affective situation so as to impose drastic measures without democratic deliberation.

In a similar direction, there are early signs that COVID-19 is being fed into a culture of fear to rejuvenate the US-centred world order, as we examined in Chapter 4 more thoroughly. In the Western world, right-wing populist leaders weaponize COVID-19 in the expectation of mobilizing popular support and marshalling all resources to restore the legitimacy of global capitalism. In doing so, they resort to Sinophobia and demonize China as a "common enemy" in the hope of reversing the multipolarization of world politics. Clearly, the US and its Western allies are concerned about the fact that their monopoly over global governance institutions such as the WHO is being challenged by China and other countries in the Global South. To reverse this situation, they invest in geopolitically isolating China from international trade and global governance by blaming China for COVID-19. For Trump, increasing Sinophobia was also exploited to radically transform the global division of labour with the pretext of "bringing manufacturing jobs back home."

Overall, this pandemic as a disaster reveals the crisis of neoliberal globalization and the ineffectiveness of US-led global governance. It creates a perfect opportunity for capitalism to launch a process of creative destruction, which has been much needed since the 2007–08 financial crisis. Interestingly, the *Economist* predicted in an article published in 1999 that the world economy would see the prospect of a new paradigm change in 2020 (*Economist* 1999). From a similar perspective, one could argue that the COVID-19 pandemic offers a suitable moment for the reorganization of markets in a way reminiscent of how the 9/11 terrorist attacks brought about the opportunity to reform the world political structure and overcome the 2001 recession. While the justification of surveillance for public emergency may perpetuate a stronger form of surveillance capitalism, it is also possible that the proliferation of distance-working technologies will lead to a deep transformation in global labour regimes and an unprecedented growth in the "precariat," which is more carefully examined in our next chapter. The precariat is understood here as a working-class stratum (rather than a social class on its own) that "consists of people living through insecure jobs interspersed with periods of unemployment or labour-force withdrawal (misnamed as 'economic inactivity') and living insecurely, with uncertain access to housing and public resources" (Standing 2014a: 16). Coupled with economic crisis and heightened competition in the labour market, distance-working technologies have great potential to endanger representation, employment, and income security by facilitating de-unionization, employment flexibility, arbitrary dismissals, wage cuts, and a lack of social security (Standing 2014b). One could thus anticipate substantial increases in household debts and work-from-home monitoring that violates workers' private lives.

REFERENCES

Agamben, G. 2020. "The Invention of an Epidemic." *European Journal of Psychoanalysis*, Feb. 26. <https://www.journal-psychoanalysis.eu/coronavirus-and-philosophers/>.

Baiman, R.P., H. Boushey, and D. Saunders. 2000. *Political Economy and Contemporary Capitalism: Radical Perspectives on Economic Theory and Policy*. London: Routledge.

Bedirhanoglu, P. 2004. "The Nomenklatura's Passive Revolution in Russia in the Neoliberal Era." In L. McCann (ed.), *Russian Transformations: Challenging the Global Narrative* (pp. 19–41). London: Routledge Curzon.

Cooney, P. 2007. "Argentina's Quarter Century Experiment with Neoliberalism: From Dictatorship to Depression." *Revista de Economia Contemporanea* 11, 1: 7–37.

Deutsche Welle. 2020a. "What Influence Does China Have over the WHO?" *Deutsche Welle*, April 17. <https://www.dw.com/en/what-influence-does-china-have-over-the-who/a-53161220>.

Deutsche Welle. 2020b. "Yuval Noah Harari on COVID-19: 'The Biggest Danger Is Not the Virus Itself.'" *Deutsche Welle*, April 22. <https://www.dw.com/en/virus-itself-is-not-the-biggest-danger-says-yuval-noah-harari/a-53195552>.

Duncan, L.A., M. Schaller, and J.H. Park. 2009. "Perceived Vulnerability to Disease: Development and Validation of a 15-Item Self-Report Instrument." *Personality and Individual Differences* 47, 6: 541–546. <https://doi.org/10.1016/j.paid.2009.05.001>.

Economist. 1999. "Catch the Wave." February 18. <https://facultystaff.richmond.edu/~bmayes/pdf/Joseph%20Schumpeter_Catch%20the%20wave.pdf>.

Furedi, F. 2018. *How Fear Works: Culture of Fear in the Twenty-First Century*. London: Bloomsbury Publishing.

Harari, Y.N. 2020. "Yuval Noah Harari: The World After Coronavirus." *Financial Times*, March 20. <https://www.ft.com/content/19d90308-6858-11ea-a3c9-1fe6fedcca75>.

Hellinger, D.C. 2014. *Comparative Politics of Latin America: Democracy at Last?* London: Routledge.

Hughes, L., and S. Payne. 2020. "Johnson Warns Public to Prepare to Lose Loved

Ones to Coronavirus." *Financial Times*, March 12. <https://www.ft.com/content/65094a9a-6484-11ea-a6cd-df28cc3c6a68>.

Klein, N. 2007. *The Shock Doctrine: The Rise of Disaster Capitalism*. New York: Allen Lane.

____. 2020. "Naomi Klein: How Big Tech Plans to Profit from the Pandemic." *The Guardian*, May 13. <https://www.theguardian.com/news/2020/may/13/naomi-klein-how-big-tech-plans-to-profit-from-coronavirus-pandemic>.

Kotz, D., and F. Weir. 2007. *Russia's Path from Gorbachev to Putin: The Demise of the Soviet System and the New Russia*. London: Routledge.

Linke, U., and D.T. Smith. 2009. "Fear: A Conceptual Framework." In U. Linke and D.T. Smith (eds.), *Cultures of Fear: A Critical Reader* (pp. 1–17). London: Pluto Press.

Lovelace, B. and D. Mangan. 2020. "White House Predicts 100,000 to 240,000 Will Die in US from Coronavirus." CNBC, March 31. <https://www.cnbc.com/2020/03/31/trump-says-the-coronavirus-surge-is-coming-its-going-to-be-a-very-very-painful-two-weeks.html>.

Mendieta, E. 2011. "The Politics of Terror and the Neoliberal Military Minimalist State: On the Inheritance of 9-11." *City* 15, 3-4: 407–413.

Montemurro, N. 2020. "The Emotional Impact of COVID-19: From Medical Staff to Common People." *Brain, Behavior, and Immunity*. <https://doi.org/10.1016/j.bbi.2020.03.032.>

Roberts, S.L. 2020. "Tracking COVID-19 Using Big Data and Big Tech: A Digital Pandora's Box." *LSE*, April 20. <https://blogs.lse.ac.uk/politicsandpolicy/tracking-covid-19/>.

Rossi, R., V. Socci, D. Talevi, S. Mensi, C. Niolu, et al. 2020. "COVID-19 Pandemic and Lockdown Measures Impact on Mental Health Among the General Population in Italy. An N=18147 Web-Based Survey." *MedRxiv*, April 9. <https://doi.org/10.1101/2020.04.09.20057802>.

Rubin, B.F. 2020. "Alexa Is More Vital Than Ever During Coronavirus, and Amazon Knows It." CNET, September 25. <https://www.cnet.com/news/alexa-is-more-vital-than-ever-during-coronavirus-and-amazon-knows-it/>.

Saad-Filho, A., F. Iannini, and E.J. Molinari. 2007. "Neoliberalism and Democracy in Argentina and Brazil." In P. Arestis and M. Sawyer (eds.), *Political Economy of Latin America: Recent Issues and Performance* (pp. 1–35). London: Palgrave Macmillan.

Soper, T. 2020. "Amazon Alexa Leader: COVID-19 Has Sparked 'a Huge Increase in the Use of Voice in the Home.'" *GeekWire*, June 25. <https://www.geekwire.com/2020/amazon-alexa-leader-covid-19-sparked-huge-increase-use-voice-home/>.

Standing, G. 2014a. *A Precariat Charter: From Denizens to Citizens*. London: A&C Black.

____. 2014b. "The Precariat-The New Dangerous Class." *Amalgam* 6, 6-7: 115–119.

Taylor, M. 2006. *From Pinochet to the 'Third Way': Neoliberalism and Social Transformation in Chile*. London: Pluto Press.

Tovey, A. 2020. "Facial Recognition System Adapted to Spot Coronavirus Victims." *The Telegraph*, April 27. <https://www.telegraph.co.uk/business/2020/04/27/

thermal-camera-identification-system-prepares-companies-life/>.

Wang, C., R. Pan, X. Wan, Y. Tan, L. Xu, et al. 2020. "Immediate Psychological Responses and Associated Factors During the Initial Stage of the 2019 Coronavirus Disease (COVID-19) Epidemic Among the General Population in China." *International Journal of Environmental Research and Public Health* 17, 5. <https://doi.org/10.3390/ijerph17051729>.

Whitehead, M. 2020. "Surveillance Capitalism in the Time of COVID-19: The Possible Costs of Technological Liberation from Lockdown." *Prifysgol Aberystwyth University Interdisciplinary Behavioural Insights Research Centre*, May 11. <https://abi554974301.wordpress.com/2020/05/11/surveillance-capitalism-in-the-time-of-covid-19-the-possible-costs-of-technological-liberation-from-lockdown/>.

Žižek, S. 2020. *Pandemic! COVID-19 Shakes the World*. New York: OR Books.

Zuboff, S. 2019. *The Age of Surveillance Capitalism: The Fight for a Human Future at the New Frontier of Power*. London: Profile Books.

③ Digital Capitalism to the Rescue of the Neoliberal Labour Regime

A Pandemic Perspective

As specified in Karl Marx's *Economic Manuscript of 1861–63*, a defining characteristic of capitalism is that "the production process is subsumed under capital ... in such a way that it is the determining, dominant mode of production" (Marx and Engels 2010: 135). Taking the cue from a Marxist account of capitalism, our previous chapter offered a thorough examination of how capitalism has been transforming in the present day. We thereby scrutinized the growing salience of digital and disaster capitalism and its broader implications for capitalists in the COVID-19 era. Much of our focus was directed towards the rise of digital platforms, the concomitant consolidation of Big Tech's monopoly power through the accelerated commodification of data and its intensifying surveillance practices for data extraction from every sphere of human experience. We also made a brief mention of how digital capitalism relegates individuals to unintentional producers of this commodity while subjugating the working class to the interests of Big Tech through an ideological discourse built on the merits of digital capitalism.

In Marx's definition of capitalism, mentioned above, a second characteristic of this socioeconomic system is that it "rests on the relation of capital and wage labour" (Marx and Engels 2010: 135). As Marx points out, there is an inextricable relation between capital and labour, since the former corresponds to "self-expanding value" that results from the exploitation of labour (Marx 1887). This is also consistent with Vladimir Ilyich Lenin's foundational definition of capitalism as "that stage of the development of commodity production at which not only the products of human labour, but human labour-power itself becomes a commodity" (Lenin 2008: 93).

Proceeding from the centrality of labour to understanding capitalism, therefore, this chapter extends our COVID-instigated analysis of digital and surveillance capitalism to labour relations.

We argue that the digital transformation of capitalism and the increasing role of surveillance in this transformation may have triggered a new phase of the neoliberal labour regime that is currently being accelerated in the COVID-19 era. By labour regimes here, we understand the prevailing modes of recruiting, mobilizing, organizing, and exploiting labour (Selwyn 2016). Understood as such, the character of labour regimes does not only shape society's production patterns, including our production systems and industrial relations, but also the order of our private ways of life and social institutions, such as the welfare and education systems (Hebel and Schucher 2006). What makes the current regime in place "neoliberal" is its reliance on the principle of flexibility and implications for precarization (Jaskulowski and Pawlak 2020).

Put differently, the neoliberal labour regime marks a "transition from secure and permanent forms of employment to a new regime characterised by different forms of insecure, casualised and flexibilised work" (Pye et al. 2012: 331). Digital capitalism and its accelerated growth under the COVID-19 conditions have further intensified flexibility with increased surveillance. Such an environment allows for unprecedented levels of surplus extraction and widescale impoverishment in economic as well as psychological and physiological respects. In what follows, we present these arguments in two sections. The first provides a conceptual framework that revisits Marx's concepts of surplus value and pauperization from a contemporary perspective into digital capitalism, precarization, and a social factory. In the second section, we apply this conceptual framework to the context of COVID-19.

Workers' Exploitation and Pauperization Under Digital Capitalism

In Marxist terminology, surplus value corresponds to the value created by the wage-worker that is greater than the cost of its labour-power and is appropriated by the capitalist. According to Marx, surplus value constitutes the major source of capital accumulation by which capital grows in size. With this in mind, he goes on to identify two basic forms in which capital accumulation occurs. The first has to do with the concentration of capital, i.e., "the increasing mass of wealth which functions as capital" (Marx 1887: 440), whereas the second involves the centralization of capital, or "concentration of capitals already formed, destruction of their individual independence, expropriation of capitalist by capitalist, transformation of many small into a few large capitals" (Marx 1887: 440). In previous chapters we have shown that with the advancement of digital technologies that enable the easy and fast commodification of data regarding every area of human experience, there is both concentration and centralization of capital in the hands of Big Tech, as it controls the online platforms as digital monopolies. Paradoxically, however, capital accumulation goes hand in hand with what Marx calls "pauperization," or the accumulation of "misery, agony of toil slavery, ignorance, brutality, mental degradation" (Marx 1887: 451). From this, Marx concludes that the growing power of capitalist monopolies intensifies socioeconomic inequalities and strengthens the position of capitalists vis-à-vis workers by various means: unbounding the possibilities for surplus value extraction, influencing public and social policies in favour of pro-business reforms, constraining employment, depreciating the value of labour power, and undermining the state of the working class in national income.

Marx distinguishes between two basic forms of exploitation that help to intensify capital accumulation at the expense of widescale pauperization: absolute and relative surplus value. In absolute surplus value, the capitalist intensifies the worker's exploitation by increasing the amount of time for work. Popular methods for maximizing absolute surplus value include extending the working day, imposing overtime work, and increasing the intensity of labour by reducing the frequency of breaks or imposing a harsher workplace discipline. As for relative surplus value, this type of surplus value is extracted by constraining earnings or the amount of time devoted to work. This can be done by the introduction of new technology and management techniques for greater productivity. Other ways of increasing relative surplus value concern wage reductions and reducing the cost of living, e.g., Asian sweatshops providing free dormitories in exchange for lower wages.

In the neoliberal context, pauperization can be systematically explained by reference to a phenomenon called the "precarization" of the working class, broadly understood as all the wage-earners who do not "own and control the capital" (Wright 2015: 189). As a major source of both relative surplus value extraction and pauperization, precarization refers to the preponderance of a minimum of seven forms of labour-related insecurity that are characteristic of neoliberal labour regimes, where the growing power of monopolies results in pro-business government regulations and a business-friendly job market at the expense of working-class interests (Standing 2011). First, the neoliberal labour regime is characterized by increased labour market insecurity in the absence of adequate earning opportunities, i.e., a lack of access to meaningful and dignifying employment in the absence of a government commitment to "full employment." This in turn creates an expanded "reserve army of labour," to use Marx's original formulation about pauperization. Second and relatedly, precarization is accelerated through income insecurity, which concerns the lack of an adequate stable income due to the preponderance of flexible employment (e.g., part-time, temporary, short-term, and self-employment), as well as the absence of protective mechanisms such as minimum wage machinery, wage indexation, comprehensive social security, and progressive taxation. Third, the working class commonly suffers from employment insecurity under the neoliberal labour regime, which leaves it vulnerable to arbitrary dismissals and management practices such as mobbing, bullying, and other kinds of workplace abuse. This problem not only contributes to the preservation of an expanded "reserve army of labour" but also to the psychological immiseration of the working class. Another form of labour-related insecurity that potentially leads to psychological immiseration speaks to job insecurity, where the worker loses "control over the content of a job and the opportunity to build a career ... in conjunction with his or her interests, training and skills" (Mojsoska and Dujovski 2018: 277). This is also related to skill reproduction insecurity, which describes the lack of opportunities for vocational training essential to workers' self-fulfillment and upward mobility. Work insecurity, or the lack of occupational health and security, constitutes the sixth form of labour-related insecurity, which potentially causes physical immiseration on the part of workers. Finally, one could argue that all of these immiserating forms of insecurity feed off representation insecurity since the absence of a collective voice by workers strengthens the position of capitalists under the neoliberal labour regime.

Under the present conditions, the digitalization of capital is mirrored in the digitalization of labour in various ways. As far as the digitalization of capital is concerned, this process translates into a myriad of processes, including companies adapting their digital infrastructure for more flexible, efficient, agile, cost-effective, and informed business models, data becoming the major commodity, and the development and widening use of cyber-physical systems. One could observe that the COVID-19 pandemic has intensified this process further, where companies that have succeeded in adopting digital technologies were able to adjust to the pandemic conditions better. Particularly, companies that provided online services and products and those that owned platforms facilitating various forms of business online were the ones that thrived. On the other hand, businesses that lack such capabilities and those sectors and companies that cannot adapt due to the nature of their products and services took a heavy blow. Having already addressed this context, here we provide a critical evaluation from a labour-centred perspective.

In previous chapters, particularly, we underlined how digital platforms of Big Tech have become digital monopolies with immense power and wealth, with surveillance of human experience at the heart of this accumulation. Here, we look at the human costs of digitalization of labour under digital capitalism and how this has intensified in the COVID-19 context. Worthy of special emphasis here is that all of this validates Marx's aforementioned observations about capital accumulation. What requires further elaboration in this chapter is how exploitation and pauperization build on each other under the conditions of digital capitalism and COVID-19. From a labour-centred perspective, it is plausible to argue that digital capitalism provides an optimal environment for the maximum extraction of surplus value at the expense of physical, psychological, and material pauperization.

The transformation of labour under digital capitalism can be best captured by reference to digital labour. In Fuchs's definition, digital labour can be understood as any type of labour performed "in a way that monetarily benefits ICT corporations," including mineral workers, ICT assemblage and manufacturing industry, knowledge workers, software engineers, workers of industrial recycling and e-waste management, and precarious service workers (Fuchs 2014: 4; 2015). Fuchs (2014) thus defines digital labour in relation to the power of and the exploitation by digital capitalists. This understanding of digital labour is not entirely different from "cognitive labour," characterized by its mental, symbolic, and communicative properties and describing information workers, programrs, ethical hackers, financial traders, alongside service and hospitality workers, telephone hawkers, and carers (Hill 2015). Worthy of note, however, is that digital labour also includes the manual workers who are employed in industrial sectors benefiting ICT (Fuchs 2014).

The digitalization of labour cannot be conceived outside the context of the automation process where some jobs are replaced by smart machines and software or carried over to digital platforms. These processes include a wide spectrum of examples from courses taught on online platforms to selling physical commodities through social media channels. Here, digitalization implies major changes in both the practice of and expectations from labour, which find its expression in what David Harvey (1990) calls "time-space compression." According to Harvey, the recent transformations of capitalism have led to a "time-space compression" characterized by the speeding-up of our pace of life and the shrinking of the world into a "small global village."

This time-space compression could also be associated with what one could call "techno-cultural acceleration," which suggests that digital capitalism has exploited the benefits of recent developments in the speed of transport and communications as part of the 4IR (Wajcman 2015).

From a pro-capitalist perspective of techno-optimism, these technological developments would be expected to increase the amount and quality of our free time for a happier and fulfilling life. However, the reality has turned out to be very different. The 4IR's technological achievements have been weaponized in the hands of digital capitalism to accelerate our working life and to intensify surplus value extraction on an unprecedented scale. This is facilitated through the diffusion of a "common obsession with novelty" combined with an "over-work culture" that legitimizes the intensification of work (Wajcman 2015). Workers are turned into "willing slaves" to the extent that they internalize the ideal type of "employee," who is supposed to embrace any kind of novelty in the name of increasing capitalist productivity and other management-defined virtues such as multitasking skills, flexibility, and business based on loosely formulated job descriptions (Wajcman 2015). These cultural values facilitated by constant (digital) connectivity also help workers consent to unpredictable, fast-paced and tight deadlines, day-long availability, and work-related events outside regular work hours.

Moreover, the intensification of surplus value extraction through accelerated precarization has led digital capitalism to entirely colonize our private lives and brought a new dimension to spiritual if not material and physiological pauperization. This situation can be vividly captured by the concept of "social factory." Digital capitalism has evolved to a point where the very essence of being human becomes a commodity, which is extracted even outside the workplace (Zuboff 2019). At this point, "the capital accumulation process escapes the confines of the factory and ... capitalism is no longer content simply to extract surplus value at the point of production from purchased labor time, but increasingly captures the (free) sociality of everyday life and turns it into surplus value" (Mumby 2020: 2). Besides remote work and its convergence with domestic labour, social factory is also embodied in "prosumption" (Fuchs 2014). This phenomenon all together represents the epitome of capitalist exploitation thanks to the maximization of surplus value extraction with minimal cost, while leading to a new wave of "pauperization" with the disappearance of leisure time and the declining quality of social reproduction.

Labour and the COVID-19 Pandemic

Previously, we addressed how the COVID-19 pandemic has intensified the digitalization of capitalism. In this section, we extend our analysis to digital labour in the COVID-19 context. This context points to a new wave of precarization in the neoliberal labour regime. For one thing, rising unemployment in all types of jobs, where workers end up with limited bargaining power, increased labour market insecurity, especially for sectors where there is minimal government support for businesses in the absence of universal basic income. Under the pandemic conditions, workers are subjected to cost-saving practices such as arbitrary dismissal, increasing employment insecurity, and reduction and flexibility in wages, which exacerbates the problem of income insecurity. The COVID-19 environment testifies to many workers receiving partial wages and "fac[ing] unemployment without being officially laid off — for example by not having contracts renewed or by seeing a reduction in working hours to zero — and thus many will not be eligible for unemployment benefits" (Matilla-Santander et al. 2021: 2). As these affect the mental and physical well-being of workers, those who work from home and lack a safe home environment will be exposed to greater risks, such as family conflicts. The already vulnerable workers who often lack access to paid sick leave "will be forced to work while sick to avoid losing income or a job, further accelerating the unequal spread of COVID-19" (Matilla-Santander et al. 2021: 2). Moreover, those who are forced to work in the workplace are at risk of being exposed to a work environment with no adequate virus control and safety measures (Matilla-Santander et al. 2021). These conditions point to increased work insecurity for employees where there is inadequate protection of their psychological and physical health and security.

At this point, it is worthwhile to note that the pandemic has highlighted the distinction between intellectual work that can be conducted mainly online, minimizing risks of physical contact, and service and manual work that necessitates physical labour, including "essential workers," such as garbage collectors, public transport drivers, and package delivery personnel, or "frontline workers," such as those in healthcare. For instance, at the manual work end of "digital labour," Amazon has been criticized for overworking its warehouse workers and for not taking adequate health precautions as the pandemic has fuelled online shopping (Bhattarai 2020). The white-collar workers who are required by employers to work physically can also be added to this group in terms of greater exposure to risk. Existing inequalities regarding class, gender, race, citizenship, and immigration status are thus reflected in the inequality of exposure to the virus. In the US, for example, "recent estimates suggest that low-income workers, non-white workers, workers with less educational attainment, and workers in service occupations are all less likely to be able to work from home than their peers," making them more vulnerable to contract the disease in their work environments as they lack the necessary PPE and workplace safety measures (O'Donnell 2020: para. 3). In the Global North, it is women, people of colour, and migrants who disproportionately work in service and manual labour (Kang et al. 2017). On a global scale, as cognitive sectors such as design, sales and marketing are concentrated in the Global North, outsourced precarious manufacturing jobs in the Global South mean, once again, that it is the members of these nations, particularly women, who become more vulnerable in terms of health risks in the workplace (Kang et al. 2017). Moreover, agricultural migrants, who work as vital actors of agri-food systems, are hit hard by the pandemic. According to the report by the Food and Agriculture Organization of the United Nations (2020), the pandemic measures including "business closures and restrictions to movement, combined with lack or limited access to all forms of social protection, increase migrants' vulnerability to poverty and food and nutrition insecurity" (2). Many of these workers, who suffer from poor housing and working conditions as well as inadequate access to healthcare or social protection due to their informal or irregular status, already face increased risk of exposure to occupational safety and health hazards. With the pandemic, the risk of contracting and spreading the virus is higher for these groups. Moreover, the report states that "measures affecting the movement of people (internally and internationally) and resulting labour shortages will have an impact on agricultural value chains, affecting food availability and market prices globally," especially affecting those who need access to affordable food worldwide (Food and Agriculture Organization of the United Nations 2020: 1).

For those workers who *are* able to socially isolate themselves, there are other factors of precarity with serious implications for exploitation and pauperization under the pandemic conditions. The new normal under COVID-19, including social isolation and mandatory lockdowns, means that remote workers are home most of the time, including nights and weekends, which are times normally beyond the visibility of employers. Under the COVID-19 context, these physical conditions, coupled with the capabilities that digital technologies provide in terms of connectivity, translate into opportunities for capital to extract more surplus value from labour. Indeed, from the employer perspective, these conditions imply that "employees" are technologically capable to work on their computers and connect to online platforms when needed.

From a capitalist perspective, the benefits of telecommuting, where the employee works from outside the workplace as a result of an employment arrangement, lie in "improvements in performance, cuts to the costs of 'home-work-home' travelling [including a reduction in carbon footprint], saving time and organizational resources, and higher employee satisfaction" (Molino et al. 2020: 2). However, from a labour-centred perspective, remote working under the pandemic conditions means that "employees" face longer and/or more intensified workdays as they work for longer hours to compensate for the lack of face-to-face work, complete work-related tasks outside working hours, and are expected to multitask between various tasks of the job as well as their work and personal lives. All of this increases work insecurity at the expense of excessive levels of exploitation. For instance, in the US, the workday has become longer, where "people worked an average of 48.5 minutes more per day, compared with the pre-virus period" (Ivanova 2020: para. 3). According to a working paper for the National Bureau of Economic Research (2020), estimates about the extra length of the workday go up to as much as three hours on average (DeFilippis et al. 2020). This is marked by a 17% increase in the number of meetings that the report shows, despite the 21% decrease in average meeting length. "At first glance, [their] finding that meetings have become shorter seems to cut against the broader pattern. … However, meeting length is not independent of meeting frequency or size. To coordinate many calendars, employees may find it necessary to shorten meetings to accommodate more frequent meetings with more attendees" (DeFilippis et al. 2020: 7). DeFilippis et al. (2020) suggest that the significant difference in length may be explained by a nonstandard work schedule, where workers are more flexible during the day to alternate between work time and breaks. However, it also becomes easier to overwork as the boundaries between work and personal life are blurred through multitasking (Ivanova 2020).

As these changes increase the absolute surplus value extracted from labour with the lengthening of the workday, they also contribute to the relative surplus value through the flexibility of these arrangements. In such cases, flexibility implies that the employee's leisure time is colonized under the employer's expectation for constant connectivity and the employee's consent in line with the ideals of the "overwork culture." Due to the capabilities that digital technologies provide, they are expected to be always available for work and to meet tight and arbitrary deadlines. As a result, this situation includes disregarding employees' other responsibilities at home. Under the COVID-19 conditions, this has particularly affected women who usually take on most of the domestic work including housework and caregiving duties (Anderson and Kelliher 2020; Hodder 2020). According to a Deloitte survey (2020) conducted with nearly 400 women across nine countries, "the number of women who say they are responsible for 75% or more of caregiving responsibilities (e.g., childcare or care of other family members) has nearly tripled to 48% during the pandemic compared to their caring responsibilities before COVID-19" (5). Moreover, 65% reported that they have more responsibility in terms of housework; 58% of those who have children reported increased childcare responsibilities and 53% of those with children reported responsibilities regarding homeschooling/education (Deloitte 2020). These are significant changes, especially when compared to the finding that nearly half of the women stated that they feel the need to be always available from a work perspective, including those women without caregiving responsibilities. In their case, the lack of these responsibilities translates to a stronger feeling of necessity to be available, creating a toll on their mental and physical well-being (Deloitte 2020). As a result, nearly 70% of the women who faced the pandemic disruptions of their routines are concerned about their career growth (Deloitte 2020).

Remote working arrangements are often praised for giving workers more autonomy over their own time and space. However, as many employees started telecommuting with the pandemic, employer surveillance has also increased under the pretext of guaranteeing full worker participation. This surveillance can be practised in a myriad of ways, including but not limited to "stamping a digital timecard" by logging into or being active on online platforms, where failure to do so at the beginning of the workday is considered as being late for work (Hern 2020). In other, more intense, forms of supervision, the employees are asked to visually check in with their employers daily where they are asked to turn their webcams on. Such requests by employers for the availability of technology for surveillance have gone to a point where "earlier this year, the consultancy PwC came under fire for developing a facial recognition tool that logs when employees are away from their computer screens while working from home" (Hern 2020: para. 13). While monitoring of employees might be considered as a necessary practice by the employers, "it undermines employees' autonomy and possibly adds to the intensity and stress of work. Worse, it erodes trust, the core of the psychological contract between workers and employers" (Riso 2020: para. 4). Moreover, it invades the privacy of the employees, especially when it is considered that even though employees might work from home, home is still considered a private space. The surveillance thus increases job insecurity for employees in that they start to yield control over the tasks belonging to their jobs.

Finally, working from home leads to isolation with both psychological and social effects. While remote working may provide a better working environment with fewer distractions, previous studies on remote working (Mann and Holdsworth 2003; Molino et al. 2020) have shown that remote working can be a strong source of stress as a result of multitasking and role conflict in addition to the pressures of constant connectivity and employer surveillance, with all factors limiting skill reproduction security by hurting productivity and autonomy. While it has been suggested (Anderson, Kaplan, and Vega 2015) that remote working can increase employee well-being, these results may be mediated by autonomy where the employees had the opportunity to choose where and how to work, rather than being forced to do so due to a pandemic (Anderson and Kelliher 2020). Furthermore, the isolation created by remote working has negative implications for employee mobilization in cases of employer violations of worker rights, leaving workers more vulnerable against exploitative practices, increasing representation insecurity of labour.

Review and Discussion

In this chapter, we discussed how the expansion of digital capitalism and its manifestations in the COVID-19 era have prompted a new wave of precarization under the neoliberal labour regime. Against the backdrop of the adaptation of digital technologies into business models and the commodification of human experience through data, digitalization of labour facilitates increased levels of exploitation and pauperization including creating a social factory of labour. The emergence of digital capitalism has contributed to the expansion and exacerbation of labour insecurities, especially in the COVID-19 environment. Adding to the existing inequalities and forms of precarious employment structured into the social organization of labour, available evidence shows that digitalization adds further reduction in workers' bargaining power, arbitrary dismissal, and wage cuts. In the case of remote working, due to constant connectivity, the workers increasingly suffer from work intensity and flexible hours, which in turn further erodes leisure time and the quality of social reproduction. Workplace safety concerns are transferred to households at the expense of serious mental and physical health issues. The disadvantaged position of remote workers cannot be conceived of separately from precarious workers forced to on-site work, whose bargaining power and working conditions are also under growing threat during the pandemic.

REFERENCES

Anderson, A.J., S. Kaplan, and R.P. Vega. 2015. "The Impact of Telework on Emotional Experience: When, and for Whom, Does Telework Improve Daily Affective Well-Being?" *European Journal of Work and Organizational Psychology* 24, 6: 882–897.

Anderson, D., and C. Kelliher. 2020. "Enforced Remote Working and the Work-Life Interface During Lockdown." *Gender in Management: An International Journal* 35, 7/8: 677–683.

Bhattarai, A. 2020. "Overworked and Exhausted, Warehouse Workers Brace for a Frenzied Holiday Rush." *Washington Post*, September 3. <https://www.washingtonpost.com/business/2020/09/03/overworked-exhausted-warehouse-workers-brace-frenzied-holiday-rush/>.

DeFilippis, E., S.M. Impink, M. Singell, J.T. Polzer, and R. Sadun. 2020. "Collaborating During Coronavirus: The Impact of Covid-19 on the Nature of Work." NBER *Working Paper Series*, 27612.

Deloitte. 2020. "Understanding the Pandemic's Impact on Working Women." *Deloitte.* <https://www2.deloitte.com/content/dam/Deloitte/global/Documents/About-Deloitte/gx-about-deloitte-understanding-the-pandemic-s-impact-on-working-women.pdf>.

Food and Agriculture Organization of the United Nations. 2020. "Migrant Workers and the COVID-19 Pandemic." <http://www.fao.org/3/ca8559en/CA8559EN.pdf>.

Fuchs, C. 2014. *Digital Labour and Karl Marx*. New York: Routledge.

____. 2015. *Culture and Economy in the Age of Social Media*. New York: Routledge.

Harvey, D. 1990. *The Condition of Postmodernity*. Malden: Blackwell Publishers.

Hebel, J., and G. Schucher. (2006). "The Emergence of a New 'Socialist' Market Labour Regime in China." GIGA *Working Papers*, 39.

Hern, A. 2020. "Shirking from Home? Staff Feel the Heat as Bosses Ramp Up Remote Surveillance." *The Guardian*, September 27. <https://www.theguardian.com/world/2020/sep/27/shirking-from-home-staff-feel-the-heat-as-bosses-ramp-up-remote-surveillance>.

Hill, D.W. 2015. *The Pathology of Communicative Capitalism*. Basingstoke: Palgrave Macmillan.

Hodder, A. 2020. "New Technology, Work and Employment in the Era of COVID-19: Reflecting on Legacies of Research." *New Technology, Work and Employment* 35, 3: 262–275.

Ivanova, I. 2020. "Coronavirus Lockdowns Are Making the Workday Longer." CBS *News*, August 5. <https://www.cbsnews.com/news/covid-19-lockdown-work-from-home-day-one-hour-longer/>.

Jaskulowski, K., and M. Pawlak. 2020. "Middling Migrants, Neoliberalism and Racism." *Journal of Ethnic and Migration Studies.*

Kang, M., D. Lessard, L. Heston, and S. Nordmarken. 2017. *Introduction to Women, Gender, Sexuality Studies*. Amherst, MA: University of Massachusetts Amherst Libraries.

Lenin. V.I. 2008. *Lenin: Collected Works*. Moscow: Progress Publishers.

Mann, S., and L. Holdsworth. 2003. "The Psychological Impact of Teleworking:

Stress, Emotions and Health." *New Technology, Work and Employment* 18, 3: 196–211.

Marx, K. 1887. *Capital Volume I*. Moscow: Progress Publishers.

Marx, K., and F. Engels. 2010. *Collected Works, Volume 30*. London: Lawrence & Wishart.

Matilla-Santander, N., et al. 2021. "COVID-19 and Precarious Employment: Consequences of the Evolving Crisis." *International Journal of Health Services*. <https://doi.org/10.1177%2F0020731420986694>.

Mojsoska, S., and N. Dujovski. 2018. "Economic Security and Economic Security Index as a Measure of Economic Security." In G. Meško, B. Lobnikar, K. Prislan, R. Hacin (eds.), *Criminal Justice and Security in Central and Eastern Europe: From Common Sense to Evidence-Based Policy-making* (pp. 274–282). Maribor: University of Maribor Press.

Molino, M., et al. 2020. "Wellbeing Costs of Technology Use during Covid-19 Remote Working: An Investigation Using the Italian Translation of the Technostress Creators Scale." *Sustainability* 12, 15: 5911.

Mumby, D. K. 2020. "Theorizing Struggle in the Social Factory." *Organization Theory* 1: 1–14.

O'Donnell, J. 2020. "Essential Workers During COVID-19: At Risk and Lacking Union Representation." *Brookings*, September 3. <https://www.brookings.edu/blog/up-front/2020/09/03/essential-workers-during-covid-19-at-risk-and-lacking-union-representation/>.

Pye, O., R. Daud, Y. Harmono, and Tatat. 2012. "Precarious Lives: Transnational Biographies of Migrant Oil Palm Workers." *Asia Pacific Viewpoint* 53, 3: 330–342.

Riso, S. 2020. "COVID-19: Fast-Forward to a New Era of Employee Surveillance." *Eurofund*, December 9. <https://www.eurofound.europa.eu/publications/blog/covid-19-fast-forward-to-a-new-era-of-employee-surveillance>.

Selwyn, B. 2016. "Global Value Chains and Human Development: A Class-Relational Framework." *Third World Quarterly* 37, 10: 1768–1786.

Standing, G. 2011. *The Precariat: The New Dangerous Class*. London: Bloomsbury Academic.

Wajcman, J. 2015. *Pressed for Time: The Acceleration of Life in Digital Capitalism*. Chicago: University of Chicago Press.

Wright, E.O. 2015. *Understanding Class*. London: Verso.

Zuboff, S. 2019. *The Age of Surveillance Capitalism: The Fight for a Human Future at the New Frontier of Power*. London: Profile Books.

4 Imperialism and the COVID-19 Pandemic

Recent Trends and Prospects

As we discussed in previous chapters, the rise of digital and surveillance capitalism plays a key role in the accelerated transformation of global capitalism in the context of the COVID-19 pandemic. This being said, these developments are not the only aspects of capitalism that have gained in salience under the current conditions. One should also not overlook the issue of imperialism, which imposes itself as an unavoidable topic when addressing global capitalism. Iranian President Hassan Rouhani (2020: par. 1), who asserted that "US imperialism [is] a more dangerous virus than corona for human society," was perhaps the first world leader to draw attention to the strengthening relevance of imperialism. We thus observe that the issue of imperialism has also spilled into public opinion debates. Serious concerns have been raised regarding the possibility of US imperialism pursuing more aggressive policies in response to its accelerated hegemonic decline and the challenge of a global pandemic (Ziauddin 2020).

David Bush (2020) draws attention to the intensification of international competition for acquiring materials and equipment used to fight the pandemic, including personal protective equipment, ventilators, drugs, and vaccines. Whilst affluent countries are wealthy enough to outspend them, poorer countries suffer from limited access to resources. Moreover, Bush sets forth the example of Iran and China to illustrate the role of imperialism in weaponizing the COVID-19 pandemic. Economic sanctions continue to undermine Iran's struggle with the pandemic by destabilizing the economy and restricting Iran's access to medical materials and equipment. In a similar vein, US imperialism attempts to obscure its historic failures to fight the pandemic by scapegoating China and intensifying its ongoing trade wars (Bush 2020). Furthermore, there are also concerns raised by agri-food activists. For example, GRAIN, an international non-governmental organization that advocates for community-controlled and sustainable food systems, takes aim at agro-imperialism, particularly when it comes to how "Nestlé's shareholders and executives awarded themselves a record dividend payout of US$8 billion in April 2020," which "would be enough to cover the average annual expenditures on health care for more than 100 million people in Africa" (GRAIN 2020). GRAIN's critique is also directed at the International Monetary Fund (IMF) and the World Bank, which "use their Covid-19 emergency funds to push countries into implementing agribusiness-friendly reforms."

These COVID-instigated debates around imperialism have also found a strong echo in scientific communities. A case in point is the *Lancet*, one of the world's oldest medical journals, which issued a call for "decolonising COVID-19." The *Lancet's* (2020) editorial outlines how Western scientific communities employ racist rhetoric and overlook the valuable experience of poorer countries in fighting public health problems. Similarly, Abraar Karan and Mishal Khan (2020) argue that affluent countries should have consulted countries in the Global South given their stronger experience in addressing public health problems. However, their experience was overlooked due to a neocolonial bias that Western countries possess moral and technical superiority over countries in the Global South.

In reality, the US health system eventually collapsed during the pandemic, and China's successful public health efforts were labelled as "draconian." Not only was China scapegoated for allegedly being the geographical origin of the pandemic, but also the US imposed a travel ban on China, even though "most of the cases in the eastern U.S. were of European origin" (Karan and Khan 2020). According to Karan and Khan, the severity of the public health situation in the Global South greatly owes to the legacy of imperialist policies, particularly that of "structural adjustment grants" offered by the World Bank. Loans offered by imperialist centres were mostly conditional on building up "the private sector rather than to strengthen essential social systems like healthcare" (Karan and Khan 2020).

In line with Karan and Khan's observations, World Health Organization Director-General Tedros Adhanom Ghebreyesus affirmed that the world is "on the brink of a catastrophic moral failure" amidst the COVID-19 pandemic. He remarked that in the world today, there is a lowest-income country where only 25 doses of COVID-19 vaccine have been administered by mid-January 2021, in stark contrast to a group of at least 49 higher-income countries where over 39 million doses of vaccine have already been administered.

According to Ghebreyesus, it is also unjust to start by allowing for the vac-cination of healthier adults in affluent countries instead of "health workers and older people in poorer countries" (Euronews 2021). Furthermore, Fernando Hellmann, Bryn Williams-Jones, and Volnei Garrafa (2020) take issue with ethical double standards in clinical research, which they associate with "moral imperialism and persistent colonialist thinking." As such, the authors denounce how trials that are considered unethical in imperialist countries are "justified in low-and-middle-income countries because the existing standards of care are less." Finally, according to Shashank Kumar and Rubén Gaztambide-Fernández (2020), the spread of the COVID-19 pandemic is entangled in the "rhythms of transnational capitalism," which have not only exacerbated socioeconomic inequalities but also further centralized power on a global scale. The authors argue that these processes reveal the increasing relevance of imperialism understood as the centraliza-tion of power over ever-expanding territories and populations at the expense of heightened inequalities and exploitation, not only of natural resources but also human labour.

Taking a cue from these COVID-instigated debates, this chapter delves into the recent transformations that have taken place in the capitalist-imperialist system. In doing so, we extend our discussion about digital and surveillance capitalism to the broader context of imperialism. By imperial-ism, we mean a historically evolving constellation of power relations that systemically govern interactions between states, monopoly-capitalist actors, and other non-state groups on a global scale (Gürcan 2021). Indeed, these relations are but a manifestation of the globalizing tendency of capitalism that determines the economic, politico-military, and cultural-ideological modes of control over raw materials, labour relations, investment oppor-tunities, and accumulation processes in the Global South. In the first place, the imperialist system is erected on a strong economic base that provides the material conditions of existence and development for global capitalism. In political terms, moreover, imperialism is embodied in the combination of geopolitical conflicts, military interventions, and economic sanctions (Gürcan 2021).

In what follows, we explore how digital and surveillance capitalism transforms the imperialist system. This is followed by an analysis of what one could call "ecological imperialism," which increases in relevance within the joint context of the COVID-19 pandemic and climate change. We then turn the spotlight onto the medical dynamics of imperialism amplified against the backdrop of the pandemic. Our chapter concludes with a discussion of the intensification of geopolitical conflicts in the COVID era.

From Digital Capitalism to Imperialism

The US information and communication technology (ICT) sector is a driving force for the contemporary imperialist system (Gürcan 2021). It is home to the world's largest companies, such as Hewlett-Packard, AT&T, Apple, IBM, and Verizon. Seven of the world's top ten software companies (Microsoft, IBM, Oracle, HP, Symantec, Activision Blizzard, and EMC) are from the US. Likewise, Dell, Intel, HP, Apple, and Cisco are US-based entities which are among the world's top ten ICT hardware companies. The same goes for Google, Microsoft, Facebook, Yahoo!, Wikimedia Foundation, eBay, Amazon, InterActive Corp, Apple Computer, and AOL, which are the world's most profitable web companies (Mirrlees 2013; Boyd-Barrett 2015; Gürcan 2021). When it comes to global desktop browser markets, the 2012 estimates suggest that US products such as Microsoft's Internet Explorer, Mozilla's Firefox (which happens to be affiliated with Time Warner's Netscape), Google's Chrome, and Apple's Safari have a market share of almost 100%. The same estimates reveal that Microsoft holds a market share of more than 90% of the global desktop operating system market for PCs. Google, Yahoo!, and Microsoft's Bing's global share of the desktop search engine market amounts to as much as 94% (Boyd-Barrett 2015). The global dominance of US-based ICT companies may therefore be the strongest arm of imperialism, particularly considering how their monopoly power not only reproduces the preponderance of American values but also fosters the growth of a "surveillance capitalism" led by digital monopolies such as Google and Facebook (Fuchs 2013).

According to Jai Vipra (2021), the monopolization of the ICT sector has led to the formation of "Big Tech," which "derives its influence from the centrality of data to the new technologies, and their exclusive control over large troves of data generated by their users." Big Tech offers a wide range of services including online advertising, personal computing, digital infrastructure and data storage, digital media and entertainment, e-commerce platforms, and automation technology. In this context, the reorganization of the world economy around a massive wave of digitization has enabled Big Tech to exert greater control over global value chains. In his report for Focus on the Global South, a prominent critical think-tank, Vipra also compiles a list of the most representative constituents of Big Tech based on market capitalization for the year 2019. Unsurprisingly, seven out of the world's top ten companies are digital technology companies and the top five digital monopolies are US-based: Microsoft, Apple, Amazon, Alphabet (Google's holding company), and Facebook. Similarly, 2018's top ten social media platforms by monthly active users include seven US-owned companies: Facebook, Youtube, Instagram, Tumblr, Google+, Reddit, and Twitter. From the point of view of imperialism, Vipra argues that Big Tech uses its strong influence within the US government and the World Trade Organization in "staving off regulations that would even the playing field and give consumers more control over their digital futures." Equally problematic for Vipra is how Big Tech works in close cooperation with the Pentagon and the CIA as business partners, whilst "the degree to which Big Tech firms use the data they store for other entities for their own benefit remains an open question."

The historical development of the US ICT sector is organically linked with the military dynamics of imperialism (Gürcan 2021). The Third Industrial Revolution originated in post-World War II military efforts at improving the traditional military functions of command, control, and intelligence by boosting research and development of advanced communications technologies (Boyd-Barrett 2015). The US military took the lead in these efforts with the close assistance of ICT giants such as IBM and AT&T, serving as military contractors. The assistance of the media-industrial complex to military imperialism also extended to media manipulation. In the Cold War era, for example, the CIA's Operation Mockingbird recruited American journalists into anti-communist manipulation in the lead of media giants such as CBS and the Time-Life empire (Boyd-Barrett 2015).

In the neoliberal era, these technological and operational efforts have also been extended to network-centric warfare through corporate contractors from the defence and ICT industries. Military contractors assisting the war efforts of US imperialism include defence technologies giants such as Lockheed Martin, Boeing, Northrup Grumman, Raytheon, and General Dynamics. This list extends to prominent ICT companies (e.g., Dell, IBM, Verizon, Sprint Nextel, AT&T, and Qwest), as the representatives of the US media-industrial complex. The Network Centric Operations Industry Consortium (NCOIC), whose founding members also include Microsoft, Hewlett-Packard, and Cisco, assumes a strategic role in these efforts in close coordination with the US government, particularly the Department of Defense and the Department of Homeland Security (Schiller 2011).

One could argue that the COVID-19 pandemic has greatly contributed to the increased relevance of Big Tech to the imperialist system. According to a McKinsey and Company report (2020), which we addressed in Chapter 1, the pandemic has accelerated the digitization of customer and supply-chain interactions as well as those of internal firm operations on a vast scale. The report forecasts that the digitization of capitalism will prove to be a long-lasting process that will not be confined to temporary solutions to

COVID-related conjunctural challenges. Digitization has already become a strong marker for competitiveness and corporate success. Furthermore, this phenomenon is designated as a strategic area that will facilitate economic recovery in the post-COVID period (Dwoskin 2020).

This being said, there appear to be strong reasons for a cautious approach when dealing with such optimism about digital capitalism, as we urged in Chapter 1. From the point of view of imperialism, one should note that Big Tech has grown powerful by exploiting the opportunity "to expand their power, crush rivals, and change their political fortunes" (Dwoskin 2020). Thanks to the pandemic conditions, "longer-term shifts in how people shop, work and entertain themselves" have occurred, which amplifies Big Tech's value to the imperialist system (Dwoskin 2020). With Big Tech companies providing essential services for consumers and governments, moreover, the pace of corruption and antitrust probes against digital monopolies has decelerated (Dwoskin 2020).

After the COVID-19 pandemic, the amplified power of monopoly capitalism in the ICT sector is likely to revitalize global capitalism and consolidate the imperialist system. In the meantime, one could observe the intensification of what has come to be known as the "digital cold war" between the US and its main rivals, China and Russia (Vipra 2021). In December 2020, for example, the US baselessly accused Russia of conducting cyberattacks that allegedly affected around 50 organizations, including "the US Treasury and Departments of Homeland Security, State and Defence" (BBC 2020). Similarly, by the end of 2020, the Trump administration revoked the licence of Huawei suppliers and blacklisted several Chinese companies, such as Xiaomi, for maintaining ties with the Chinese military (*South China Morning Post* 2021).

The COVID-19 Pandemic and Ecological Imperialism

Digital and surveillance capitalism is not the only contributor to the rising relevance of imperialism in the context of the COVID-19 pandemic. When addressing imperialism under these conditions, one should also take into consideration other salient aspects related to the ecological, medical, and geopolitical dynamics of imperialism. In this section, we focus on the concept of "ecological imperialism." Climate change and the COVID-19 pandemic are often viewed as converging crises that stem from a shared causality and generate mutually reinforcing effects. Perhaps most importantly, both phenomena are caused by environmentally detrimental human activity and result in "the preventable loss of lives through actions that are delayed, insufficient, or mistaken" (*Lancet* 2021). Therefore, they require joint responses "to improve public health, create a sustainable economic future, and better protect the planet's remaining natural resources and biodiversity" (*Lancet* 2021). Meanwhile, the opportunity to formulate progressive policy responses is used as a pretext to launch comprehensive reforms to revitalize global capitalism, which are evaluated in our next chapter in greater depth. If the objective is to revitalize global capitalism, however, this calls for caution regarding the potential realignments in the imperialist system after the COVID-19 pandemic.

Ecological imperialism can be defined as "the subjugation of the economic, political, and/or social institutions of a (generally peripheral) country for the biophysical, metabolic needs of the (generally core or semi-periphery), inextricable from the purpose of making such resources accessible and amenable (in the right quantities and for the right price) to the needs of (foreign) capital accumulation" (Frame 2016). This form of subjugation is particularly directed at ensuring the flow of biophysical resources from peripheral environments to imperialist centres. Ultimately, the socioeconomic and environmental burdens of the imperialist system are placed on the shoulders of marginalized groups and subjugated states, which usually represent the populations most affected by economic and environmental disasters.

In the neoliberal era, ecological imperialism drew its power mainly from what David Harvey calls "accumulation by dispossession," simply understood as the centralization of wealth and power through imperialist pillaging (Harvey 2010; Milios and Sotiropoulos 2009; Gürcan 2021). Indeed, the privatization of the environment and extractivism served as core mechanisms for accumulation by dispossession. Exemplary of such mechanisms is the privatization of water resources in Bolivia (1997–2001) and Argentina's transgenic soy extractivism to the detriment of its food sovereignty and ecological sustainability (Olivera and Lewis 2004; Gras and Hernandez 2014). Such mechanisms of accumulation hold a destructive potential for both the economy and the environment, which renders economic and environmental crises inevitable. To postpone or resolve these crisis tendencies, global capitalism often resorts to spatio-temporal fixes, which express "capitalism's insatiable drive to resolve its inner crisis tendencies by geographical expansion and geographical restructuring" (Harvey 2001: 24). With the accelerated crisis of neoliberal capitalism amidst the COVID-19 pandemic, therefore, capitalists are considering the possibility of "socioecological" and "technological" fixes by redeploying sustainable technologies and boosting sustainable industries as "a new source of profit and investment" (Frame 2016: 89–91; McCarthy 2015).

At the end of the day, these fixes are likely to fuel a new wave of ecological imperialism in the post-COVID era. When lead firms based in imperialist countries place stronger sustainability demands on their suppliers from the Global South, suppliers will be forced to compensate their constrained profit margins by compromising their "social sustainability," i.e., by cutting labour costs and worsening work conditions (Ponte 2019). Another potential impact of such fixes can be observed in the intensification of "green" and "blue" grabbing efforts as a form of accumulation by dispossession, by which land and marine areas are expropriated by profit-seeking foreign actors. When these grabbing efforts are conducted for the declared purpose of "conservation" and "ecotourism," they are most likely to be "transformed in 'spectacle' for the enjoyment of the wealthy," particularly those from imperialist countries (Ponte 2019). Land grabbing for biofuel production and other monocultural practices, which are deceptively deemed "sustainable," would ultimately undermine both the economic and ecological well-being of countries in the Global South (Ponte 2019). One should also take into account the possibility that imperialist countries may attempt to hastily impose a one-track framework of green capitalism on countries in the Global South to preserve their hegemonic position. Particularly, the transfer of green capital and technology to the Global South may be rendered conditional on certain political premises and expectations to preserve this hegemonic position under a unified system of control and discipline in a way similar to structural adjustment programs. Given that imperialist countries retain a head-start advantage in "international trade, the international division of labour, acquisition of natural resources, and use of environmental pollution space," the globalization of green capitalism designed after the material interests of imperialism may end up impeding the development of countries in the Global South (Qingzhi 2017).

The COVID-19 Pandemic and Medical Imperialism

The COVID-19 pandemic also raises particular concern about what one could call "medical imperialism," i.e., how imperialist interests are advanced in the sphere of medical and health services through the mediation of international institutions such as imperialist states, pharmaceutical monopolies, philanthropic foundations, international financial institutions, international trade agreements, and international health organizations (Waitzkin and Jasso-Aguilar 2015). One important aspect of medical imperialism is the influence of powerful pharmaceutical companies such as Johnson & Johnson, Novartis, Roche, Pfizer, Sanofi, Merck, GSK, AstraZeneca, Bayer, AbbVie, Lilly, and Bristol-Myers Squibb (O'Rioardan 2017). In the case of COVID-19, pharmaceutical companies, as part of one of the most profitable industries in the world economy, have conducted their research thanks to the massive financial support provided by governments (Gaffney, Himmelstein, and Woolhandler 2020). For example, AstraZeneca's vaccine research was heavily supported by Oxford University and public funding. The same goes for BioNTech, which enjoyed the German government's backing (Lapavitsas 2021), which is worth at least $443 million (Attard 2020), adding to $118 million in loans offered by the European Investment Bank. Moreover, the Trump administration launched Operation Warp Speed to provide $10 billion in funding for private sector efforts at developing COVID-19 vaccines. Of this funding, $2.5 billion went to Moderna. Britain provided a similar amount of funding for six pharmaceutical companies (Murphy 2020). Oxford/AstraZeneca alone benefited from £84 million in funding from the UK government (Attard 2020).

This very situation reflects the centrality of the "medical-industrial complex" as the driving force of medical imperialism. Here, the medical-industrial complex can be understood as interlocking relationships between the private health sector (e.g., powerful pharmaceutical companies, insurance companies, and private hospitals), academia, and government (Burlage and Anderson 2018). This interlocking relationship raises serious ethical issues, especially with academics serving in managerial positions as part of both universities and pharmaceutical companies as well as executives of pharmaceutical companies serving in public task forces and regulatory bodies (Lexchin 2018). This adds to pharmaceutical companies hiring academics or physicians as "opinion leaders" or paying medical researchers for publishing articles based on company-owned and manipulated data (Lexchin 2018).

The "intellectual property rights" regime serves as a core mechanism of "accumulation by dispossession" for imperialism (Harvey 2010), which is imposed by the World Trade Organization, which delivers harsh trade sanctions when its rules are violated. Big Pharma is a main beneficiary of the imperialist intellectual property rights regime alongside agri-food monopolies ("Big Food") and Big Tech. As part of this regime, COVID-19 vaccines and medication developed in imperialist centres have become a major source of revenue for pharmaceutical companies (Sell 2020). It is highly problematic to see how these companies use public funding to produce public goods to be sold for astronomical prices. Estimates suggest that two-thirds of spending on health research relies on public funding and "every new drug approved in the U.S. [between 2010 and 2016] had been funded by the state (totalling $100 billion of public money) before being patented by companies" (Murphy 2020). This begs the questions of why access to these products is on a commercial basis and why pharmaceutical profits are not channelled back into public research in meaningful amounts (Attard 2020). One should bear in mind that pharmaceutical companies generate astronomical revenues from the sale of medical products and services. Remdesivir, which is used to treat COVID-19, is sold for over US$3000, even though its cost of production is estimated at US10$ (Lupkin 2020).

Another important aspect of medical imperialism concerns corporate militarism and states. Regarding corporate militarism, the medical-industrial complex has developed interlocking relations with the military-industrial complex as the driving force of military imperialism. A strong case in point is Johnson & Johnson, whose board "includes the CEO of Lockheed Martin, the chairman of Rolls-Royce, a board member of Boeing, and a board member of Honeywell" (Barker 2020). Besides corporate militarism, leading states in the imperialist system have engaged in fierce competition with one another, especially in the COVID era. This competitive attitude has impeded any attempt at establishing strong coordination mechanisms on a global scale (Lapavitsas 2021). In the meantime, it is estimated that affluent states have stockpiled a large number of COVID-19 vaccines to the extent that as many as "70 lower-income countries will only be able to vaccinate one in 10 people" at best in the medium term (Attard 2020).

The COVID-19 pandemic has also brought forth concerns about imperialist philanthropy. Quite conveniently, it turns out that the Bill and Melinda Gates Foundation (BMGF) has been funding research on the mRNA technology since 2014, which happens to be the main technology behind the Moderna and Pfizer-BioNTech vaccines (Kluger 2020). With the outset of the COVID-19 pandemic, BMGF took the lead in realigning the global health agenda and became one of the largest contributors to Access to COVID-19 Tools Accelerator, a global cooperation initiative to facilitate private business efforts at COVID-19 testing, treatment, and vaccination in collaboration with national governments and hegemonic international institutions (Lapavitsas 2021). As "the largest philanthropy organisation worldwide focusing on public health" (Waitzkin and Jasso-Aguilar 2015), BMGF's general approach is geared towards prioritizing the role of corporate actors by mobilizing philanthropic and state support (Birn and Richter 2018; Birn 2014). Worthy of note here is that BMGF also has an agenda for globalizing "green capitalism," which gains relevance in the COVID-19 period. In 2006, BMGF established the Alliance for a Green Revolution in Africa (AGRA). AGRA seeks to promote transgenic agriculture and the integration of African agriculture into global value chains rather than ensure African food security. It collaborates with African governments to encourage African small farmers to purchase expensive "inputs such as hybrid seeds and synthetic fertilizers via agrochemical companies" (Urhahn 2020). In turn, agrochemical companies coerce African small farmers into producing export-oriented monocultural crops such as corn and soy at the expense of their food sovereignty (Thompson 2012; Urhahn 2020). Indeed, these attempts cast serious doubt on the prospects of not only medical imperialism but also green capitalism as an important agenda that imposes itself in the COVID period.

The Intensification of Geopolitical Conflicts Amidst the COVID-19 Pandemic

The digital, ecological, and medical dynamics of imperialism are all important in shaping post-COVID capitalism. However, our understanding of recent realignments in the imperialist system would remain incomplete without due consideration of geopolitical dynamics. In this regard, one cannot help but notice that the imperialist system is experiencing tectonic changes, which have been leading to major economic and political instabilities since the early 2000s. Arguably, among the most important transformations is the crisis of hegemonic governance and a rapidly growing geopolitical multipolarization. The year 2008 marked a turning point in this process, where the explosion of the US sub-prime bubble in 2008 triggered a worldwide economic crisis that shook the American world order to its very foundations. The waves from this crisis were strongly felt in Europe, with a sudden disappearance of economic growth, accompanied by rising unemployment. This protracted socioeconomic crisis was accompanied by another crisis, this time of a political nature, which helped to paralyze the European integration process: the Brexit referendum result in 2016. As a result, the EU has lost much of its attractiveness as a role model for global governance. This has undermined the Western-centric world order at the expense of the principle of institutional regulation (Gürcan 2019a; 2019b).

The crisis of global economic governance was particularly noticeable in the 2017–18 NAFTA dispute, during which the United States insisted on renegotiating NAFTA and threatened to withdraw from the agreement (Gürcan 2019b). Similarly, the United States had proposed to create the Trans-Pacific Partnership, which was intended to become the world's largest trade deal as a US-led countervailing measure against China's growing influence over the Asia-Pacific region (Pham 2017). However, in 2017 the Trump administration decided to withdraw from the agreement, leading many countries to further question US global leadership. Added to this is the fact that the North Atlantic Treaty Organization (NATO) is currently undergoing one of its deepest crises since its creation in 1949, especially with the intensified US-German debate on the NATO budget and Turkey's alienation from the alliance. The severity of the NATO crisis was explicitly acknowledged by President Emmanuel Macron of France, who observed: "What we are currently experiencing is the brain death of NATO" (*Guardian* 2019: par. 2).

Ultimately, the implosion of hegemonic governance in almost every major sphere of cooperation has made countries in the Global South question the legitimacy of the US-led world order (Gürcan 2019b). Following the 2008 crisis, the BRICS alliance (Brazil, Russia, India, China, and South Africa) emerged as a platform to voice Global South countries' growing concerns and interest in taking an active part in global governance. In particular, China and Russia have become major and rising forces in geopolitical multipolarization by building alternative institutions for global governance. Among the most salient institutions are the Collective Security Treaty Organization (CSTO), the Shanghai Cooperation Organization (SCO), the Eurasian Economic Union (EAEU), and the Asian Infrastructure Investment Bank (AIIB). Another important development in this regard is the creation of the Belt and Road Initiative (BRI) in 2013, which is a China-led initiative consisting of infrastructure, resource, and investment development networks, intended to be active in over 152 countries across Asia, Europe, Africa, the Middle East, and the Americas (Gürcan 2020).

Events and developments in the year 2020 indicate that the COVID-19 pandemic has accelerated the destabilization of the imperialist system by intensifying geopolitical conflicts in favour of increased multipolarity. For one thing, US imperialism has not lost its aggressive character despite Donald Trump's claim of being "the first president in decades who has started no new wars" (France 24 2021). On the contrary, Trump's foreign policy exposed the contradictions of imperialism even further. According to political analyst Bill Schneider, Trump might have been "the most pro-Israel president since Harry Truman recognized Israel" (Hjelmgaard 2019). The Abraham Accords process — which marked the first official normalization of relations between Arab countries and Israel since 1994 — is deemed "Trump's signature foreign policy achievement" (Jakes 2020). Trump recognized Jerusalem as Israel's capital and the Golan Heights as part of Israeli sovereignty, while also supporting Israel's settlement activity in the West Bank (Lazaroff 2021). After withdrawing from the Joint Comprehensive Plan of Action, an agreement to ensure Iran's adoption of an exclusively peaceful nuclear energy program, the Trump administration extended its economic sanctions against Iran, which has had crippling effects on the Iranian economy under 2020's pandemic conditions (Lazaroff 2021). During the pandemic, Trump (Lee and Goodman 2021) also intensified US economic sanctions against Cuba, Venezuela, and Nicaragua.

The pandemic could not prevent the further escalation of the US-China trade wars, either. Quite the contrary, as Michael Howell, CEO of Crossborder Capital asserts, these conflicts are likely to evolve into a larger-scale conflict that involves a "capital, trade and technology war" (Taylor 2020) during the pandemic. Worthy of note here is that Trump's military policies did not radically diverge from those of his predecessors. For instance, it is estimated that US troop strength has been kept at roughly the same level as at the end of Obama's final term in office (Benjamin and Davies 2020). This adds to the fact that "the reduction of troops was much greater under President Obama (Giles 2020), as both large-scale deployments in Iraq and Afghanistan ended during his years in charge." Overall, US military expenditure rose by over 14% in the period 2016–19 under the Trump administration, from around US$640 billion to over US$731 billion (Sipri n.d.).

Review and Discussion

Our discussion in this chapter revealed that imperialism is ever more relevant in the COVID-19 era. Particularly relevant are aspects of imperialism that concern the digital, ecological, medical and geopolitical dimensions of world politics. In previous chapters, we addressed the increasing relevance of digital and surveillance capitalism. Here, we extended our discussion to how monopolies in the ICT sector have become part of the world's largest group of companies and started to exert global influence at an unprecedented pace. This process has certainly gained considerable momentum with the COVID-19 pandemic. Besides developing interlocking relations with military imperialism, what one could call "Big Tech" is colonizing data and expanding its influence, not only on the US government but also on international institutions such as the WTO. In close partnership with leading military actors such as the Pentagon and the CIA, Big Tech's growing influence serves to revitalize global capitalism and lay the ground for a digital cold war.

Regarding ecological imperialism, the agenda of revitalizing global capitalism seems to be implemented in tandem with the fight against the pandemic and climate change. There is reason to argue that this fight is not rooted in naïve intentions. The COVID-19 environment provides a strong ground for implementing "socioecological" and "technological" fixes through the deployment of pro-capitalist policies for environmental sustainability. This, however, could gestate the formation of a new hegemonic system of control and discipline in the imperialist system. The global implementation of green capitalism may contribute to increased efforts at land grabbing while creating an enabling environment for conditional technology and capital transfers to the Global South. Suppliers in the Global South risk being pulled into new patterns of unequal relations by being forced to compromise their social sustainability to comply with the new sustainability requirements imposed by imperialist countries.

The case of medical imperialism bears strong similarities to that of digital imperialism in that Big Pharma, as a state-backed formation interlocked with economic and military interests, has acquired new momentum during the COVID-19 pandemic. In this conjuncture, we observe the consolidation of the imperialist intellectual property rights regime, which points to the deployment of a new phase of accumulation by dispossession. While accelerating the corporate cooptation of academia and science, this process also brings to the fore private sector–driven solutions with the backing of not only governments but also philanthropic organizations that impose a profit-driven system of health and agriculture in tandem. As a result, the pandemic period testifies to the intensification of international rivalry and competition rather than cooperation. The unrestrained commodification of COVID-19 medication and vaccines also results in constrained medical access in the Global South.

Finally, we point to the geopolitical dynamics of imperialism. The COVID-19 pandemic has sharpened the contradictions of the imperialist system. We testify to the intensification of geopolitical rivalries and increased multipolarity. These developments find their strongest expression in the onset of an all-out "capital, trade, and technology war," which is accompanied by rising US military spending and geopolitical aggression against Global South countries such as Iran, Venezuela, and Cuba.

REFERENCES

Attard, J. 2020. "COVID-19 Vaccines: Big Pharma Profits Trump Human Lives." *Marxist*, December 22. <https://www.marxist.com/covid-19-vaccine-big-pharma.htm>.

Barker, M. 2020. "Coronavirus and Profiteering: Pills for Need Not Profit." *Socialist Alternative*, April 24. <https://www.socialistalternative.org/2020/04/24/coronavirus-and-profiteering-pills-for-need-not-profit/>.

BBC. 2020. "US Cyber-Attack: Around 50 Firms 'Genuinely Impacted' by Massive Breach." *BBC*, December 20. <https://www.bbc.com/news/world-us-canada-55386947>.

Benjamin, M., and N. Davies. 2020. "Trump's Record on Foreign Policy: Lost Wars, New Conflicts, and Broken Promises." *Jacobin*. <https://jacobinmag.com/2020/06/donald-trump-war-iraq-iran-syria-afghanistan-obama-bush>.

Birn, A.E. 2014. "Philanthrocapitalism, Past and Present: The Rockefeller Foundation, the Gates Foundation, and the Setting(s) of the International/Global Health Agenda." *Hypothesis*, 12, 1: e8.

Birn, A.E., and J. Richter. 2018. "US Philanthrocapitalism and the Global Health Agenda: The Rockefeller and Gates Foundations, Past and Present." In H. Waitzkin (ed.), *Health Care under the Knife: Moving beyond Capitalism for Our Health* (pp. 155–174). NYU Press.

Boyd-Barrett, O. (2015). *Media Imperialism*. Sage Publications.

Burlage, R., and M. Anderson. 2018. "The Transformation of the Medical-Industrial Complex: Financialization, the Corporate Sector, and Monopoly Capital." In H. Waitzkin (ed.), *Health Care Under the Knife: Moving Beyond Capitalism for our Health* (pp. 69–82). NYU Press.

Bush, D. 2020. "Imperialism and COVID-19." *Spring*. <https://springmag.ca/imperialism-and-covid-19>.

Dwoskin, E. 2020. "Tech Giants Are Profiting—and Getting More Powerful—Even As the Global Economy Tanks." *The Washington Post*, 27.

Euronews. 2021. "'Catastrophic Moral Failure': WHO Chief Slams COVID Vaccine Rollout." *Euronews*, January 18. <https://www.euronews.com/2021/01/18/catastrophic-moral-failure-who-chief-slams-covid-vaccine-rollout>.

Frame, M. 2016. "The Role of the Semi-Periphery in Ecologically Unequal Exchange: A Case Study of Land Investments in Cambodia." In Harry F. Dahms, Paul K. Gellert, R. Scott Frey (eds.), *Ecologically Unequal Exchange* (pp. 75–106). Palgrave Macmillan.

France 24. 2021. "Trump Touts Record of 'No New Wars,' Standing Up to China in Farewell Address." *France 24*. <https://www.france24.com/en/americas/20210119-trump-touts-record-of-no-new-wars-standing-up-to-china-in-farewell-address>.

Fuchs, C. (2013). *Social Media: A Critical Introduction*. Sage.

Gaffney, A., D.U. Himmelstein, and S. Woolhandler. 2020. "COVID-19 and US Health Financing: Perils and Possibilities." *International Journal of Health Services*, 0020731420931431.

Giles, C. 2020. "US Election 2020: Has Trump Kept His Promises on the Military?" *BBC News*, October 16. <https://www.bbc.com/news/election-us-2020-54060026>.

GRAIN. 2020. "Agro-Imperialism in the Time of Covid-19." *Committee for Abolition of Illegitimate Debt*, July 16. <http://www.cadtm.org/Agro-imperialism-in-the-time-of-Covid-19?utm_source=dlvr.it&utm_medium=facebook>.

Gras, C., and V. Hernández. 2014. "Agribusiness and Large-Scale Farming: Capitalist Globalisation in Argentine Agriculture." *Canadian Journal of Development Studies/ Revue canadienne d'études du développement* 35, 3: 339–357.

Guardian. 2019. "Macron Criticised by US and Germany over NATO 'Brain Death' Claims." <https://www.theguardian.com/world/2019/nov/07/macron-warns-of-nato-brain-death-as-us-turns-its-back-on-allies>.

Gürcan, E.C. 2019a. *Multipolarization, South-South Cooperation and the Rise of Post-Hegemonic Governance*. Routledge.

____. 2019b. "Building a Fair World Order in a Post-American Age." *Belt & Road Initiative Quarterly* 1, 1: 6–16.

____. 2020. "The Construction of 'Post-Hegemonic Multipolarity' in Eurasia: A Comparative Perspective." *The Japanese Political Economy* 46, 2–3: 127–151.

____. 2021. *Imperialism After the Neoliberal Turn*. New York: Routledge.

Harvey, D. 2001. "Globalization and the 'Spatial Fix.'" Geographische Revue Zeitschrift für Literatur und Diskussion 3, 2: 23–30.

____. 2010. *The New Imperialism*. Oxford: Oxford University Press.

Hellmann, F., B. Williams-Jones, and V. Garrafa. 2020. "COVID-19 and Moral Imperialism in Multinational Clinical Research." *Archives of Medical Research*.

Hjelmgaard, K. 2019. "Israel Settlements: Donald Trump Proves He's the 'King of Israel.'" *USA Today*, November 19. <https://www.usatoday.com/story/news/world/2019/09/16/donald-trump-israel-election/2333266001/>.

Jakes, L. 2020. "Trump Incentives for Signing Peace Accords with Israel Could Be at Risk." *New York Times*, December 20. <https://www.nytimes.com/2020/12/20/us/politics/trump-israel-sudan-peace-accord.html>.

Karan, A., and M. Khan. 2020. "The Ghosts of Colonialism Are Haunting the World's Response to the Pandemic." *National Public Radio*, May 29. <https://www.npr.org/sections/goatsandsoda/2020/05/29/862602058/opinion-the-ghosts-of-colonialism-are-haunting-the-worlds-response-to-the-pandem>.

Kluger, J. 2020. "What Bill Gates Thinks About the State of the Fight Against COVID-19." *Time*, December 22. <https://time.com/5923916/bill-gates-covid-19-letter/>.

Kumar, S., and R. Gaztambide-Fernández. 2020. "Are We All in This Together? COVID-19, Imperialism, and the Politics of Belonging." *Curriculum Inquiry* 50, 3: 195–204. doi: 10.1080/03626784.2020.1819525.

Lancet. 2020. "Decolonising COVID-19." <https://www.thslancet.com/journals/langlo/article/PIIS2214-109X(20)30134-0/fulltext>.

____. 2021. "Climate and COVID-19: Converging Crises." Vol 397, January 9. <https://www.thelancet.com/journals/lancet/article/PIIS0140-6736(20)32579-4/fulltext>.

Lapavitsas, C. 2021. "How Capitalist Competition Hobbled the COVID-19 Vaccine Rollout." *Jacobin*, January 6. <https://jacobinmag.com/2021/01/capitalist-competition-covid-19-vaccine-rollout>.

Lazaroff, T. 2021. "Ten Gains, Losses for Israel under US President Donald Trump." *The Jerusalem Post*, January 20. <https://www.jpost.com/american-politics/ten-gains-losses-for-israel-under-us-president-donald-trump-656054>.

Lee, M., and J. Goodman. 2021. "Trump Hits Cuba with New Terrorism Sanctions in Waning Days." *AP News,* January 11. <https://apnews.com/article/joe-biden-mike-pompeo-cuba-venezuela-foreign-policy-41ddf75b0c13d290cd539d90e62 27b0a>.

Lexchin, J. 2018. "The Pharmaceutical Industry in Contemporary Capitalism." *Monthly Review* 69, 10: 37–50.

Lupkin, S. 2020. "Remdesivir Priced at More Than $3,100 for a Course of Treatment." *National Public Radio,* June 29. <https://www.npr.org/sections/health-shots/2020/06/29/884648842/remdesivir-priced-at-more-than-3-100-for-a-course-of-treatment>.

McCarthy, J. 2015. "A Socioecological Fix to Capitalist Crisis and Climate Change? The Possibilities and Limits of Renewable Energy." *Environment and Planning A* 47, 12: 2485–2502.

McKinsey and Company. 2020. "How COVID-19 Has Pushed Companies over the Technology Tipping Point—And Transformed Business Forever." <https://www.mckinsey.com/business-functions/strategy-and-corporate-finance/our-insights/how-covid-19-has-pushed-companies-over-the-technology-tipping-point-and-transformed-business-forever>.

Milios, J., and D.P. Sotiropoulos. 2009. "Classical Theories of Imperialism: A New Interpretation of Capitalist Rule, Expansionism, Capital Export, the Periodization and the 'Decline'of Capitalism." In *Rethinking Imperialism: A Study of Capitalist Rule* (pp. 9–32). London: Palgrave Macmillan. <https://doi.org/10.1057/9780230250642_2>.

Mirrlees, T. (2013). *Global Entertainment Media: Between Cultural Imperialism and Cultural Globalization.* Routledge.

Murphy, D. 2020. "Big Pharma and the Search for a Vaccine." *Green Left Weekly* 1290 (Nov. 26). <https://www.greenleft.org.au/content/big-pharma-and-search-vaccine>.

Olivera, O., and T. Lewis. 2004. *Cochabamba!: Water War in Bolivia.* South End Press.

O'Riordan, L. 2017. *Managing Sustainable Stakeholder Relationships.* Springer Verlag.

Pham, P. 2017. "Why Did Donald Trump Kill This Big Free Trade Deal?" *Forbes,* December 29. <https://www.forbes.com/sites/peterpham/2017/12/29/why-did-donald-trump-kill-this-big-free-trade-deal/?sh=28a0b7c64e62>.

Ponte, S. 2019. "Green Capitalism and Unjust Sustainabilities." *Samfundsøkonomen* 4: 102–108.

Qingzhi, H. 2017. "Criticism of the Logic of the Ecological Imperialism of 'Carbon Politics' and Its Transcendence." *Social Sciences in China* 38, 2: 76–94.

Rouhani, H. 2020. "US Imperialism a More Dangerous Virus than Corona for Human Society/Emphasis on the Need for Cooperation Between the Two Countries in OPEC Plus to Restore Oil Price Stability." *President.* <http://www.president.ir/EN/114725>.

Sell, S. K. 2020. "What COVID-19 Reveals About Twenty-First Century Capitalism: Adversity and Opportunity." *Development* 1–7.

Schiller, D. (2011). "The Militarization of US Communications." In J. Wasko, G. Murdock, & H. Sousa PhD (Eds.), *The Handbook of Political Economy of Communications* (pp. 264-282). Blackwell Publishing Ltd.

SIPRI. n.d. "SIPRI Military Expenditure Database." <https://www.sipri.org/

databases/milex>.

South China Morning Post. 2021. "Trump Slams China's Huawei, Blocking Supplies from Intel and Others, Insiders Say." January 18. <https://www.scmp.com/news/world/united-states-canada/article/3118109/trump-slams-chinas-huawei-blocking-supplies-intel>.

Taylor, C. 2020. "Coronavirus Is Accelerating a 'Capital War' Between China and the US, Investor Warns." CNBC, May 27. <https://www.cnbc.com/2020/05/27/coronavirus-is-accelerating-a-us-china-capital-war-investor-says.html>.

Thompson, C.B. 2012. "Alliance for a Green Revolution in Africa (AGRA): Advancing the Theft of African Genetic Wealth." *Review of African Political Economy* 39, 132: 345–350.

Urhahn, J. 2020. "Bill Gates's Foundation Is Leading a Green Counterrevolution in Africa." *Jacobin,* December 27. <https://jacobinmag.com/2020/12/agribusiness-gates-foundation-green-revolution-africa-agra>.

Vipra. J. 2021. "Big Tech: The Global Economy: Primer." *Global South,* January. <https://focusweb.org/wp-content/uploads/2021/01/Big-Tech-Jan2021.pdf>.

Waitzkin, H., and R. Jasso-Aguilar. 2015. "Imperialism's Health Component." *Monthly Review* 67, 3: 114.

Ziauddin, A.A. 2020. "US Imperialism in the Wake of Covid-19." *Daily Star,* May 30. <https://www.thedailystar.net/opinion/news/us-imperialism-the-wake-covid-19-1906336>.

5 From the "Great Reset" to the "Green New Deal"

Is a Reformed Capitalism Possible After COVID-19?

The COVID-19 pandemic has provoked widespread questioning of neoliberal capitalism. Even within mainstream economists and business elites, there are increasing efforts at radically restructuring global capitalism and doing away with the neoliberal paradigm. These efforts are strongly epitomized by those of the World Economic Forum (WEF), which is considered to be the hegemonic bedrock of global capitalism. The WEF was created in 1971 by Klaus Schwab, an influential business policy expert. It later evolved from a forum for European CEOs into a large corporate-elite network that brings together global capitalists, high-ranking politicians, and heads of hegemonic international organizations such as the International Monetary Fund (IMF) and the World Bank (Carroll and Sapinski 2016). This network was also extended to include mainstream academics, media professionals, artists, and civil society leaders. They are called the "Davos elite," named after the city that hosts the WEF's annual meetings. In the meantime, the WEF also holds regional meetings appealing to local elites from Global South countries or regions, such as China, India, and Africa.

The WEF meetings set the agenda for global capitalism through issue-based councils that monitor global trends and provide policy recommendations to address global risks in strategic areas, including economics, geopolitics, science, sustainability, and health (Carroll and Sapinski 2016). The WEF has assumed a similar role during the COVID-19 pandemic and its proposal for a so-called "Great Reset of Capitalism" has gained considerable traction in global media. Meanwhile, it is worthwhile to note that the Great Reset proposal has found its counterpart among left-of-centre capitalist reformers under the name of the "Green New Deal," which is voiced not only by Keynesian circles and heterodox economists but also by liberal establishment politicians, such as Ed Markey, a US politician who happens to have supported the 2003 war on Iraq, and democratic socialists, such as Alexandria Ocasio-Cortez.

All these discussions about resetting capitalism and stimulating a "New Deal" point to a more than 100-year-old dilemma of "reform or revolution," revolving around the question of whether capitalism can be reformed or not. In her influential pamphlet entitled *Social Reform or Revolution?* (1899), Rosa Luxemburg famously took up this issue and denounced the capitalist reformers who reject the necessity of revolution:

> Instead of taking a stand for the establishment of a new society, they [i.e., people who pronounce themselves in favour of the method of legislative reform in place and in contradistinction to the conquest of political power] take a stand for surface modifications of the old society. If we follow the political conceptions of revisionism, we arrive at the same conclusion that is reached when we follow the economic theories of revisionism. Our program becomes not the realisation of socialism, but the reform of capitalism; not the suppression of the wage labour system but the diminution of exploitation, that is, the suppression of the abuses of capitalism instead of suppression of capitalism itself.

Proceeding from Luxemburg's skepticism about capitalist reformism, this chapter undertakes a critical appraisal of mainstream proposals to reform the global economic system in the post-COVID era. In the first two sections, we explore the main themes underlying the WEF's "Great Reset" proposal and the Keynesian "Green New Deal." The third section critically evaluates the reformist character of these proposals by reference to the notions of green capitalism and ecological imperialism. Our conclusion provides an eco-socialist blueprint to transcend capitalist reformism in the post-COVID era.

The Great Reset of Capitalism: Reforming Capitalism Beyond Neoliberal Orthodoxy

COVID-19: *The Great Reset* — a book co-authored by the WEF's Klaus Schwab and French economist Thierry Malleret (2020) — became one of 2020's most debated books and dominated the COVID-related discussions on reforming capitalism. While the Great Reset proposal was presented to the public by Prince Charles, world leaders such as Justin Trudeau, Joe Biden, and Boris Johnson have also adopted a pro-reform discourse that approximates the Great Reset (Inman 2020; Wherry 2020). The Great Reset acknowledges that the COVID-19 pandemic has brought about a global crisis of unparalleled magnitude which exposes "the fault lines of the world, most notably social divides, lack of fairness, absence of cooperation, failure of global governance and leadership" (Schwab and Malleret 2020: 8). According to Schwab and Malleret, this crisis will have far-reaching consequences beyond the economy alone and extend to the political as well as social and geopolitical fields. To face up the challenges of a post-COVID world, the authors propose a paradigm shift that would help capitalism to get back on its feet again. This proposed shift focuses on five main areas at the macro level, namely economic, societal, geopolitical, environmental, and technological.

What Schwab and Malleret (2020: 28) call an "economic reset" challenges the "tyranny of GDP growth." In their view, economics needs a new compass for measuring progress. Accordingly, one should take better account of economic resilience by reference to a number of key determinants, such as institutionalization, infrastructure, human capital, emergency capital reserves, innovation ecosystems, and sustainability. Adding to this, the authors also urge that policy-makers should adopt new goals of public policy to address the problem of income and wealth inequality along with decreasing living standards and social welfare. This inclusive agenda is to incorporate several happiness indicators, such as accessible healthcare, mental health, child poverty, and family violence. Furthermore, Schwab and Malleret contend that this economic reset should unlock the potential of digital capitalism to revitalize the global economy based on a technologically driven and innovation-led approach. In this regard, the authors urge that the value created in the digital economy should be regarded as another compass for tracking economic progress. This is also the reason why GDP calculations are to be revised to incorporate the digital economy. Another important compass proposed by Schwab and Malleret concerns the development of a green economy and the stimulation of investments in social areas such as education and health, which are hoped to revitalize not only the innovatory dynamics of capitalism but also job creation.

Societal reset addresses the negative effects of COVID-19 on rising inequalities and social unrest, which call for the return of "big government" (Schwab and Malleret 2020: 38). Schwab and Malleret draw attention to the fact that the COVID-19 pandemic has exacerbated and exposed societal inequalities. This situation is also reflected in labour conditions where "the upper and middle classes were able to telework and self-school their children from their homes (primary or, when possible, secondary, more remote residences considered safer), while members of the working class (for those with a job) were not at home and were not overseeing their children's education, but were, instead, working on the front line to help save lives (directly or not) and the economy — cleaning hospitals, manning checkouts, transporting essentials, and ensuring our security" (35). Similarly, Schwab and Malleret point out that low-income groups and vulnerable populations, such as poverty-stricken African American communities and the homeless in the US, have been heavily affected by the pandemic, particularly when it comes to deaths from COVID-19. This is conducive to widescale popular unrest, namely violent crimes, riots, and anti-government protests, which can only be eased through "enhanced protection for workers" and "a broader, if not universal, provision of social assistance, social insurance, healthcare, and basic quality services" (41).

Schwab and Malleret also call for a geopolitical reset to confront rampant right-wing nationalism and the intensified Sino-US rivalry. Relatedly, they point to the heightened risk of deglobalization, which may result in greater regionalization and accelerated divides between North America, Europe, and Asia. Particularly concerning to Schwab and Malleret is how national leaders have so far focused on national responses to the pandemic at the expense of international cooperation. This is clearly illustrated in the US disengagement from the World Health Organization during the pandemic. In particular, the pandemic has exposed the erosion of US soft power with the failure of the Trump administration to respond to a global emergency of epic proportions:

> While in the past the US was always the first to arrive with aid where assistance was needed (like on 26 December 2004 when a major tsunami hit Indonesia), this role now belongs to China... In March 2020, China sent to Italy 31 tons of medical equipment (ventilators, masks and protective suits) that the EU could not provide. (50)

Schwab and Malleret acknowledge that the "US has stumbled in the pandemic crisis and its influence has waned" (52).This also resonates with their previous argument about economic reset: the pandemic may well contribute to the eroding dominance of the US dollar, even though there are no real alternatives to replace US financial hegemony yet.

As for the environmental reset, Schwab and Malleret reveal an important policy dilemma of the post-COVID-world. One possibility is that, driven by pandemic-related economic challenges, low oil prices, and corporate greed, world governments may prioritize economic recovery over policies targeting climate change. Another is the likelihood that governments may take advantage of the emergence of "a new social conscience among large segments of the general population that life can be different" (58) to seize the moment for introducing a green economy. Such an outcome depends on the presence of enlightened leadership, heightened risk-awareness, the development of a societal attitude towards "greener living," and increased activism (58–60).

A final area where Schwab and Malleret envision widescale reform is technology, where the pandemic has increased the relevance of robots, artificial intelligence, and tracking systems. The authors are optimistic about the pandemic accelerating the digital transformation of the global economy. This is particularly evident in how pandemic conditions have enabled "online work, education, shopping, medicine, and entertainment" (62), which are likely to acquire permanence in the post-COVID era. In the meantime, Schwab and Malleret caution about the rapid growth of digital surveillance systems given that they are vulnerable to "cyber intrusions, issues of trust in the operator of the system, and the timing of data retention" (65).

Overall, the Great Reset — as a hegemonic proposal that appeals to the Davos elite — puts forth a new model of green capitalism developing a more human and inclusive approach to the capitalist economy. Schwab and Malleret call for the return of "big government," which is hoped to accelerate the digitization of capitalism and technological innovations. Big government is also expected to address socioeconomic disparities and ease rising social tensions under COVID-19 conditions. Moreover, the Great Reset identifies several big challenges that require careful consideration. Many of these challenges speak to those explored in our previous chapters, particularly concerning the digitization of capitalism, the transformation of labour relations, the rise of surveillance capitalism, and the multipolarizarion of world politics.

Towards a Green New Deal?
The Revival of Keynesianism After COVID-19

The global appeal of the calls for reformed capitalism has not emerged with the COVID-19 pandemic. These calls had already gained added urgency following the 2007–08 economic crisis, which was considered to be the gravest economic crisis since the Great Depression. Ultimately, the Green New Deal became the driving slogan of such calls. While the idea of a Green New Deal was already being voiced by the US Green Party since the early 2000s (Atkin 2019), Thomas L. Friedman's (2007) article "A Warning from the Garden" helped to popularize this idea. Later, President Obama incorporated the idea into his platform. Moreover, in 2008, British Keynesians organized around the Green New Deal Group (GNDG) and the New Economics Foundation took the lead in public advocacy for a Green New Deal. They issued an influential report entitled *A Green New Deal: Joined-Up Policies to Solve the Triple Crunch of the Credit Crisis, Climate Change and High Oil Prices* (Green New Deal Group 2008). This proposal was later adopted by the United Nations Environment Program (UNEP) and European politicians such as Gordon Brown and Green members of the European Parliament (Pettifor 2019).

Similar to the Great Reset proposal, the idea of a Green New Deal has been gaining currency in the COVID-19 conjuncture. An Organisation for Economic Co-operation and Development (OECD) policy brief underlines that the COVID-19 pandemic has unveiled "the importance of environmental health and resilience as a critical complement to public health" (OECD 2020: par. 9). Whilst the pandemic is expected to lead to a decline in global carbon emissions and air pollution and an improvement in water quality, it has revealed a new waste management challenge and the significance of human interference with biodiversity. The policy brief accentuates that rebuilding the global economy increasingly depends on building resilience against future shocks and improving general well-being. Besides mere environmental concerns, the brief accentuates the potential of green economies to create new job opportunities, accelerate innovation, and address inequalities in tandem (OECD 2020).

South Korea has taken a critical step in implementing the Green New Deal. In July 2020, Korean President Moon Jae-in launched the so-called Korean New Deal, which promises US$135 billion investment in green and digital technology in response to the pandemic. According to this plan, over 87% of this investment comes from the government, whereas the rest is assumed by the private sector. As part of the Green New Deal, Korea prioritizes the expansion of solar panels, wind turbines, micro-grid communities, electric vehicles, hydrogen-powered fuel-cell electric vehicles, and energy efficiency policies. These priority areas are hoped to generate "green jobs" (Sung-Young, Thurbon, Tuo and Mathews 2020; OECD 2020).

GNDG's 2008 report provides a comprehensive intellectual foundation for the Green New Deal. Worthy of notice is that the report proceeds from basic Keynesian tenets, from which mainly follow two priority areas: addressing the problems of unemployment and declining demand:

This [the Green New Deal] entails re-regulating finance and taxation plus a huge transformational program aimed at substantially reducing the use of fossil fuels and, in the process, tackling the unemployment and decline in demand caused by the credit crunch. (Green New Deal Group 2008: 2)

The main idea here is to use public expenditure primarily to the benefit of domestic companies, which are hoped to allow for technological innovations and wage increases while contributing to creating environment-friendly consumption:

Any public spending should be targeted so that domestic companies benefit, and then the wages generated create further spending on consumer goods and services. So combined heat-and-power initiatives generate income for construction and technological companies, and then workers' salaries are spent on food, clothes, home entertainment, the theatre and so on, creating demand for those industries. (27)

The GNDG report states that the 2007–08 crisis cannot be reduced to a unidimensional phenomenon. This rather stems from a combination of overlapping emergencies that find their strongest expression in "a credit-fuelled financial crisis, accelerating climate change and soaring energy prices underpinned by an encroaching peak in oil production" (2). According to the report, the ultimate solution to this crisis lies in restructuring our financial, taxation, and energy systems, which can be summarized in nine points: adopting a low-carbon energy system, creating "green-collar jobs" by shifting the focus of the economy away from the financial sector and consumerism, ensuring more realistic fossil fuel prices, increasing smart investments for the development of energy-efficient innovation and infrastructure, imposing tighter controls on the domestic financial sector, forcing demergers for large banking and finance groups, restricting the international financial sector, regulating derivative products and other exotic instruments, and fighting corporate tax evasion.

Interestingly enough, the report praises Cuba's historic success in building climate resilience, transitioning into organic agriculture, and achieving food self-sufficiency through small-farming and urban agriculture:

The Cuban approach thoroughly contradicts the model of development normally sponsored by international financial institutions.

It is highly managed, focused on meeting domestic needs rather than export-oriented, largely organic and built on the success of small farms. It is so different that it has been called the "anti-model" by the World Bank, but with some startled respect. At least one analyst suggests that the Cuban experiment "may hold many of the keys to the future survival of civilisation." (31)

In her book entitled *The Case for the Green New Deal* (2019), the GNDG-affiliated economist Ann Pettifor offers a more detailed account of the Green New Deal proposal. The book puts forth a comprehensive and inclusive strategy while keeping with basic Keynesian tenets of encouraging investments and managing demand:

> We called for a sustained program to invest in and deploy energy conservation and renewable energies, coupled with effective demand management. (Pettifor 2019: 43)

Pettifor argues that this proposal aspires to more than mere behavioural, community, and technological change. It requires (inter)governmental changes through a radical transformation of economic and ecological systems. She attributes the current economic and ecological crises to financial deregulation, where limitless credit encouraged environmentally unsustainable consumerism. In a way similar to Schwab and Malleret's (2020) Great Reset, she problematizes US imperial power, epitomized in the pre-eminence of the US dollar, and critiques Obama's support for Wall Street. She does not even restrain from arguing that "dollarized financial capitalism shifted offshore has undermined the power of democratic governments and local communities to develop economic policies to meet urgent needs" (Pettifor 2019: 31). Finally, according to Pettifor, the Green New Deal relies on a set of seven principles: the adoption of a steady-state economy characterized by sustainable policies, a needs-based approach that excludes consumerism, the principle of self-sufficiency by which countries in the Global South can be freed from "colonial chains," the adoption of a mixed economy, the implementation of labour-friendly policies, monetary and fiscal coordination, and the dispensation of growth-led economic models. Pettifor believes that these principles should be mobilized to globalize the Green New Deal.

The Green New Deal idea has found a strong echo in the US Democratic Party. In February 2019, Senator Edward J. Markey and Representative Alexandria Ocasio-Cortez presented a Green New Deal resolution to the

US Senate and the House of Representatives (Ocasio-Cortez et al. 2019). Similar to Pettifor, their resolution observes that the US is undergoing a multifaceted crisis characterized by declining life expectancy and quality. The crisis finds its expression not only in climate change but also in the people's limited access to "clean air, clean water, healthy food, and adequate health care, housing, transportation, and education" (Ocasio-Cortez et al. 2019: 3). This is all attributed to wage stagnation, deindustrialization, and anti-labour policies. The resolution goes on to emphasize that the US is responsible for as high as 20% of global greenhouse emissions despite its technological capabilities in place. Therefore, "the United States must take a leading role in reducing emissions through economic transformation" (3). In this context, the policy imperatives are to create high-wage green jobs, build green infrastructure, enable access to basic human needs, promote sustainable agriculture, and fight ethno-racial oppression.

The Green New Deal gives voice to the aspirations of environmental Keynesianism while sharing striking similarities with the Great Reset. It seems that the Green New Deal discourse as a hegemonic paradigm has been adopted by several important figures in world politics in a way cognisant of the Great Reset's appeal to the Davos elite. The Green New Deal draws on a critique of neoliberalism and its finance-centred policy outlook, which is designated as the main culprit of the current crisis and accelerated by the COVID-19 pandemic. Similar to the Great Reset, the Green New Deal proposes a diversified and inclusive agenda of "big government," which however prioritizes the interests of the private sector. The main focus of this agenda is on revitalizing capitalism by stimulating employment and consumption with recourse to "green" means. Meanwhile, it is surprising to see how environmental Keynesianism calls for self-sufficiency in the name of breaking the yoke of neocolonialism (or imperialism) over the Global South, while explicitly praising Cuba for its historic successes. However, this rather "Third Worldist" praise by environmental Keynesianism contradicts its dogmatic insistence on preserving the capitalist-imperialist system and brings to mind the practical possibility of abandoning capitalism for a "more thoroughgoing and self-consistent" (Veltmeyer and Rushton 2012: 150) alternative simply called "socialism."

Green Capitalist Futures:
Global Hegemony and Ecological Imperialism

The COVID-triggered discussions around the Green New Deal raise the question of the viability of Keynesianism in bringing about the desired transformations. One should note that environmental Keynesianism mainly draws its inspiration from the experience of the US New Deal era (1933–45) and its extended impact between the 1950s and 1960s. When Franklin D. Roosevelt rose to the presidency, US politics was marked by widespread protests and the so-called rising threat of socialism in reaction to Great Depression (1929–33) conditions (Panitch and Gindin 2012). Faced with these challenges, Roosevelt encouraged the adoption of "social values more noble than mere monetary profit" (Franklin D. Roosevelt, quoted in Panitch and Gindin 2012: 55). Thereby, he pointed to the need for the state to undertake a stronger agenda of regulatory and social reforms to save capitalism from itself. He relied on the slogans, "sane radicalism" and "reform if you would preserve" (55).

At least two important issues stand out in the Rooseveltian idea of enacting a "great class compromise." One is that this compromise was originally conceived as a radical, albeit temporary measure that imposed itself amidst the advance of socialism. After all, this compromise was not essentially compatible with the profit-maximizing nature of capitalism, driven by an endless quest for capital accumulation. Roosevelt was explicit about the temporality and instrumental function of the New Deal:

> There is no question in my mind that it is time for the country to become fairly radical for at least one generation. History shows that where this occurs occasionally, nations are saved from revolutions. (55)

Ultimately, this brings up the question of not only whether capitalism is reformable at all, but also whether a "greened" version of reformed capitalism is possible in the context of COVID-19.

The second issue is that the radical restructuring of capitalism along reformist lines had shaped the world imperialist system at first hand. One should note that Roosevelt himself was not against the idea of foreign military interventionism. In his critique of the unilateral applications of the Monroe Doctrine in Latin America, he acknowledged the need for re-framing US interventionism within a multilateral framework "in the name of all the Americas and only in cooperation with other republics" (56). Even more important in this regard is how "domestic interventionism" of the New Deal era was later extended to "international interventionism" in pursuit of imperialist gains (Panitch and Gindin 2012: 63). In internationalizing the New Deal, US imperialism developed a multilateral framework around the Bretton Woods system in 1944. As part of this system, what came to be known as the Bretton Woods Institutions, the World Bank and the International Monetary Fund (IMF) and later the General Agreement on Tariffs and Trade (GATT), served to advance US global hegemony. As described by Leo Panitch and Sam Gindin (2012: 74), "the historic significance of the Bretton Woods Agreement is that it institutionalized the American state's predominant role in international monetary management as part and parcel of the general acceptance of the US dollar as the foundation currency of the international economy." These efforts at launching global capitalism were combined with the Marshall Plan, which empowered US banks and corporations in reconstructing postwar Western Europe and easing social unrest to impede the spread of socialism. As such, Europe adopted "forms of production and accumulation which had been developed earlier in the US" alongside "US-style productivist labor relations" (Panitch and Gindin 2012: 100). In the process, global Keynesianism grew into an oil-fuelled imperialist project led by US oil companies and the military. Moreover, global Keynesianism resulted in a US-led internationalized financial structure with the creation of the Eurodollar market (Panitch and Gindin 2012). In the final analysis, the history of US imperialism in what one could call the "Keynesian era" brings up the question of whether the implementation of a Green New Deal, or the Great Reseat, could trigger a new phase of imperialist expansion.

The reformability of capitalism seems highly questionable from a Marxist point of view, which problematizes green capitalism, greenwashing, and ecological imperialism. Green capitalism can be understood here as "the broad swathe of environmental politics that take the political-economic system of capitalism and its dominant institutions for granted and posit that the negative ecological impacts of exploitative economic activities can be addressed adequately by better state policies and regulation enforcement, adjustments to market and industry operations, improvements in science and the use of technology, increased knowledge and education, the work of environmental NGOs, and/or the voluntary actions of businesses and individuals" (Holleman 2018: 74–75). Even green capitalism proponents admit that this form of reformed capitalism will lead to the emergence of a new accumulation regime through so-called "path-breaking" policy reforms such as the 2015 Paris Climate Agreement and other policy actions for the development of low-carbon capitalism in the energy, industrial, and agricultural sectors (Guttmann 2018: 57).

Considering that "the primary aim of capitalist production is the accumulation of capital" (Graham 2019: 20), one could deduce that green reforms to capitalism will inevitably lead to new processes of commodification and exploitation. Moreover, one cannot but ask to what extent such reforms would be deepened in terms of improving both social justice and sustainability (Graham 2019). As framed by the Great Reset and Green New Deal proposals, green capitalism proposes an exceedingly ambitious, and even socialistic program that even targets wealth inequality. If we were to be convinced that this inclusive framework is not part of a mere public relations (PR) campaign to restore the hegemony of global capitalism, its radical proposals such as achieving wealth equality should have been detailed with greater rigour. It may even be the case that the slogan of green capitalism was redeployed to take advantage of the pandemic conditions to accelerate the advance of digital capitalism and the green corporate agenda. In this respect, it has been suggested that the adaptation of digital technologies in many individual and organizational endeavours, such as efficient distribution of physical resources, organization of production systems, and enabling of remote working, would have positive results for the environment by reducing carbon footprints and eliminating unnecessary resource use (LaBerge et al. 2020). As discussed in previous chapters, however, these evaluations often ignore the societal costs of such changes, especially in terms of labour exploitation and pauperization.

This, in turn, brings to mind the phenomenon of "greenwashing," understood as "disinformation from organizations seeking to repair public reputations and further shape public images" (Bowen 2014: 21). Greenwashing is often employed by corporate actors. Emblematic of greenwashing efforts is "We Agree," Chevron's ad campaign which sought to convey the impression that the company mobilizes community support for sustainable development. In reality, however, community leaders were selected via casting calls. The idea was to distract public opinion from the company's poor environmental and human rights record (Bowen 2014). Another exemplar of greenwashing is how ExxonMobil released funds totalling $16 million in the period 1998–2005 directed at right-wing think-tanks and scientific bodies claiming to be neutral despite their organic ties to the carbon industry. The aim there was to support research that whitewashes the negative environmental effects of the carbon industry (Wall 2010). Similarly, eco-labelling is often exploited by certain companies to misdirect consumers that their goods are more environmentally friendly than those of their competitors (Markham, Khare, and Beckman 2014). On a systemic level, the framing of biofuels as an ecological alternative constitutes a grave act of greenwashing given that it requires destructive monocultural practices at the expense of domestic food security, the devastation of rainforests, and excessive use of fertilizers and pesticides. This adds to the fact that biofuels emit a similar amount of CO_2 to petroleum fuels (Wall 2021). In green capitalism, finally, the scale of greenwashing is elevated from the level of individual corporate actors to the whole system.

It is apparent that public expenditures under green capitalism prioritize "private economic gain" and put forth superficial treatments such as increased spending on environmentally friendly industries and technologies, green employment generation, and boosting consumption (Blackwater 2012: 51, 58, 71–72). One could expect such priorities to eventually overshadow radical demands for income and wealth equality, while the pre-eminence of private gains would constrain substantial equality gains. For one thing, consumption-driven strategies are still "predicated on 'supermaterialization' at the macro scale" (Graham 2019: 24). Moreover, very little is said by green capitalism proponents when it comes to transforming power relations in production and the ownership of the means of production. If we were to somehow socialize the means of production in fossil- and carbon-intensive industries, there also arises the possibility to extend this socialization attempt to other industries, including logistics, sales and services, office work, healthcare, and education (Graham 2019; Sica 2020). Clearly, such a possibility is not conceivable within the confines of capitalism.

Another important question to address in the COVID-19 conditions is whether healthcare and R&D can be nationalized to break the monopoly of corporate power. Furthermore, it is possible to argue that no substantial gains can be achieved unless knowledge is decommodified beyond the intellectual property rights regime (Wall 2010). This is particularly important for environmentally friendly technologies and the pharmaceutical sector in a context where the pandemic is instrumentalized to develop a hegemonic framework of green and digital capitalism. Otherwise, political power and economic resources would be further concentrated in the hands of technocratic and economic groups (Graham 2019).

Finally, if the Great Reset and Green New Deal policies were to successfully "tame" capitalism, policy-makers should also be able to redress its imperialist tendencies, particularly in the environmental sphere. Theoretically speaking, however, this constitutes an impossible task given that imperialism is an intrinsic feature of modern capitalism, which finds its expression also in the globalization of the New Deal in the Keynesian era, as was discussed earlier in this chapter. An important question thereby arises regarding the viability of the Green New Deal in the post-COVID era: could this New Deal resolve the contradictions of imperialism merely through reforms?

The answer is not difficult. In the present day, US military imperialism is "the country's single largest user of fossil fuels" (Wall 2010: 95). US imperialism controls several military bases in more than 150 countries, an important portion of which are devoted to controlling oil supplies in the Middle East (Wall 2010). Currently, US military expenditure accounts for almost 50% of global military expenditure, and the contribution of NATO to global military expenditure stands as high as 70% (Golub 2010). The estimated cost of the US invasions of Iraq and Afghanistan alone are around $4.4 trillion (Creswell 2019: 484). One should emphasize that excessive military expenditure by US imperialism also represents the greatest impediment to increased public expenditure aimed at social development and ecological transition. Unsurprisingly, the Obama administration witnessed "the largest domestic oil production increase during any presidency in U.S. history," despite Obama's reformist rhetoric favouring the Green New Deal (Holleman 2018: 31). It follows that no reform can eliminate US imperialism. Similarly, it is highly doubtful that green-capitalist rhetoric can reverse the global land rush for food, water, and energy security as well as Western corporate extractivism in the Global South (Frame 2016).

In concluding this section, a final remark about imperialism is in order. As discussed in our previous chapter, capitalism uses spatio-temporal fixes to resolve its contradictions by launching new campaigns of geographical expansion (Harvey 2001: 24). Faced with one of the gravest economic crises since the Great Depression, we observe that the imperialist system is in critical need of generating new accumulation opportunities on a global scale. In this regard, it is possible to argue that the Great Reset and Green New Deal policies will serve as a socioecological and technological fix for the imperialist system.

In the final analysis, therefore, one could argue that the Great Reset and Green New Deal proposals build on the "sane radicalism" of the New Deal era, where policy-makers adopted temporary reforms to preserve capitalism and fight socialism. These reforms were later deployed to an international setting to advance the interests of US imperialism. In the post-COVID world, the deepening crisis of the capitalist-imperialist system requires the deployment of a new set of reforms that promote a similar kind of "sane radicalism." As such, green capitalism is used as part of a systemic greenwashing campaign to postpone the demise of capitalism and restore its global hegemony by launching a new phase of capital accumulation and consumerism through an environmental and technological fix. The new "big government" rhetoric does not specify the extent of socialization and nationalization required. At the end of the day, private rather than collective gains reside at the centre of this hegemonic construct, which is why it would be plausible to conclude that the inclusive and pro-labour discourse of this construct only serves a decorative function to motivate the working class.

Review and Discussion

The COVID-19 pandemic has rekindled global initiatives for reforming capitalism. Having been adopted by global elite circles, the Great Reset and Green New Deal proposals take the lead in these reformist initiatives. The real question that imposes itself is: What are we to make of these reform initiatives? There can be very little doubt that what will happen in the post-COVID era is a question of political power and class struggle rather than temporary fixes and comforting surface-level rhetoric. The unfolding of these factors will determine who will control the so-called "big government" and whose interests will be prioritized at the governmental level. Indeed, any solution that excludes anti-capitalism and anti-imperialism is doomed to function as a temporary fix and is likely to serve the hegemonic restoration of global capitalism in the longer term.

The blueprint for an alternative to capitalist reformism can be derived from eco-socialist thinking, which relies on "democratic ecological planning" in partnership with a socialist state and communities representing the working masses (Wall 2010; Löwy 2018). Full-scale nationalization is needed here for strategic sectors such as energy and mining, infrastructure, transportation, communication, defence, medicine and healthcare, and education. In this framework, large-scale decisions will be subjected to planning, whereas workers' self-management will take the initiative in smaller-scale decisions regarding issues such as local restaurants, groceries, small shops, or artisan enterprises. In line with our critique of digital capitalism and capitalist labour in previous chapters, technology will be subordinated, not to profit motives, but rather to satisfying our authentic needs (e.g., "water, food, clothing, housing, and basic services such as health, education, transport, and culture") and creating free time rather than intensifying work and unemployment (Löwy 2018: 4).

REFERENCES

Atkin, E. 2019. "The Democrats Stole the Green Party's Best Idea." *The New Republic,* February 22. <https://newrepublic.com/article/153127/democrats-stole-green-partys-best-idea>.

Bowen, F. 2014. *After Greenwashing: Symbolic Corporate Environmentalism and Society.*

Cambridge: Cambridge University Press.

Blackwater, B. (2012). "Two Cheers for Environmental Keynesianism." *Capitalism Nature Socialism*, 23(2), 51-74.

Carroll, W., and J. Sapinski. 2016. "Neoliberalism and the Transnational Capitalist Class." In S. Springer, K. Birch and J. MacLeavy (eds.), *Handbook of Neoliberalism* (pp. 39–49). New York: Routledge.

Creswell, M. 2019. "Wasted Words? The Limitations of U.S. Strategic Communication and Public Diplomacy." *Studies in Conflict & Terrorism* 42, 5: 464–492.

Frame, M. 2016. "The Neoliberalization of (African) Nature as the Current Phase of Ecological Imperialism." *Capitalism Nature Socialism* 27, 1: 87–105.

Freidman, T. 2007. "A Warning from the Garden." *New York Times*, January 19. <https://www.nytimes.com/2007/01/19/opinion/19friedman.html>.

Golub, P.S. 2010. *Power, Profit and Prestige: A History of American Imperial Expansion*. London: Pluto Press.

Graham, S. 2019. "'Green Capitalism': A Critical Review of the Literature." *Revolutionary Socialism in the 21th Century*. <https://www.rs21.org.uk/wp-content/uploads/2019/03/S-Graham-Green-capitalism-RR-15-16-March-2019.pdf>.

Green New Deal Group 2008. "A Green New Deal: Joined-Up Policies to Solve the Triple Crunch of the Credit Crisis, Climate Change and High Oil Prices." <https://neweconomics.org/uploads/files/8f737ea195fe56db2f_xbm6ihwb1.pdf>.

Guttmann, R. 2018. *Eco-Capitalism: Carbon Money, Climate Finance, and Sustainable Development*. London: Palgrave Macmillan.

Harvey, D. 2001. "Globalization and the 'Spatial Fix.'" *Geographische Revue Zeitschrift für Literatur und Diskussion* 3, 2: 23–30.

Holleman, H. 2018. *Dust Bowls of Empire: Imperialism, Environmental Politics, and the Injustice of "Green" Capitalism*. London: Yale University Press.

Inman, P. 2020. "Pandemic Is Chance to Reset Global Economy, Says Prince Charles." *The Guardian*, June 3. <https://www.theguardian.com/uk-news/2020/jun/03/pandemic-is-chance-to-reset-global-economy-says-prince-charles>.

LaBerge, L., C. O'Toole, J. Schneider, and K. Smaje. 2020. "How COVID-19 Has Pushed Companies over the Technology Tipping Point—And Transformed Business Forever." McKinsey & Company, Oct. 5. <https://www.mckinsey.com/business-functions/strategy-and-corporate-finance/our-insights/how-covid-19-has-pushed-companies-over-the-technology-tipping-point-and-transformed-business-forever>.

Löwy, M. 2018. "Why Ecosocialism: For a Red-Green Future." *Great Transition Initiative*, December. <https://greattransition.org/publication/why-ecosocialism-red-green-future>.

Luxemburg, R. 1899. *Social Reform or Revolution?* London: Militant Publications.

Markham, D., A. Khare, and T. Beckman. 2014. "Greenwashing: A Proposal to Restrict its Spread." *Journal of Environmental Assessment Policy and Management* 16, 4: 1–16.

Ocasio-Cortez, et al. 2019. "H. Res. 109 (Recognizing the duty of the Federal

Government to create a Green New Deal)." <https://www.congress.gov/116/bills/hres109/BILLS-116hres109ih.pdf>.

OECD. 2020. "OECD Policy Responses to Coronavirus (COVID-19): Making the Green Recovery Work for Jobs, Income and Growth." <https://www.oecd.org/coronavirus/policy-responses/making-the-green-recovery-work-for-jobs-income-and-growth-a505f3e7/>.

Panitch, L., and S. Gindin. 2012. *The Making of Global Capitalism: The Political Economy of American Empire*. New York: Verso.

Pettifor, A. 2019. *The Case for the Green New Deal*. New York: Verso Books.

Schwab, K., and T. Malleret. 2020. *COVID-19: The Great Reset*. Forum Publishing.

Sica, C. 2020. "For a Radical Green New Deal: Energy, the Means of Production, and the Capitalist State." *Capitalism Nature Socialism* 31, 4: 34–51.

Sung-Young, K., E. Thurbon, H. Tuo, and J. Mathews. 2020. "South Korea's Green New Deal Shows the World What a Smart Economic Recovery Looks Like." *The Conservation*, September 9. <https://theconversation.com/south-koreas-green-new-deal-shows-the-world-what-a-smart-economic-recovery-looks-like-145032>.

Veltmeyer, H., and M. Rushton. 2012. *The Cuban Revolution as Socialist Human Development*. Hollanda: Brill.

Wall, D. 2010. *The Rise of the Green Left Inside the Worldwide Ecosocialist Movement*. London: Pluto Press.

Wherry, A. 2020. "The 'Great Reset' Reads Like a Globalist Plot With Some Plot Holes." *CBC*, November 28. <https://www.cbc.ca/news/politics/great-reset-trudeau-poilievre-otoole-pandemic-covid-1.5817973>.

6 Postcapitalist Horizons for a Post-COVID World

The COVID-19 pandemic has gravely exposed the deepening crisis of global capitalism and, therefore, triggered heated debates over the necessity for a far-reaching paradigm shift in the global economy. In our previous chapter, we critically examined radical reform proposals advanced by "capitalist roaders," i.e., reformers who represent global capitalist interests. With this chapter, we show that this debate also extends to left-wing circles that question the viability of capitalism itself. Whilst the pro-capitalist debate is confined to a critique of neoliberal interpretations of capitalism within the framework of the Great Reset and Green New Deal proposals, the predominant theme among left-wing circles is "postcapitalism."

A case in point is Yanis Varoufakis, former finance minister for Greece's Syriza-led government, who calls for "a post-capitalist economy in which the markets for real goods and services no longer coordinate economic decision-making" (2020). Similarly, Anitra Nelson argues that the pandemic has revealed not only the weaknesses of capitalism but also society's potential for increased "solidarity, collaborative relationships, respect, care, and sharing" (2020: 308). Therefore, Nelson underlines that this crisis has created an enabling environment for questioning capitalism and transcending the "capitalist law of value" beyond monetary relations and private property, which we critically examined in Chapter 3. In turn, Stephen Healy and colleagues focus on the pandemic's implications for our global food systems, particularly in terms of heightened food insecurity. They argue that the accelerated crisis of our food systems under the pandemic has increased the relevance of "commons thinking." According to them, thereby, the main essence of postcapitalist imaginaries lies in remobilizing communities as "active collaborators" against the neoliberal logic of privatization and unsustainability (Healy, Chitranshi, Diprose, et al. 2020: 3). In the case of food security, postcapitalism requires the combination of active state support with the mobilization of local producers and social enterprises such as food relief charities (Healy et al. 2020).

Taking the cue from these debates, the present chapter develops a critical analysis of left-wing alternatives to capitalist reformism to provide insights into a tentative revolutionary program that could take advantage of the COVID-19 environment to defeat and transcend capitalism. Erik Olin Wright's *How to Be an Anticapitalist in the Twenty-First Century* (2019) provides one of the most comprehensive and recent accounts of the essential methods used and widely discussed by left-leaning circles in challenging capitalism. Therefore, we frame this discussion by reference to Wright's classification of six different strategies: smashing capitalism, dismantling capitalism, taming capitalism, resisting capitalism, escaping capitalism, and, finally, eroding capitalism.

The first three strategies in Wright's classification are evaluated in the next section. We put into question Wright's non-revolutionist stance that gives higher credit to reformist alternatives and recontextualize revolutionary alternatives against the backdrop of the COVID-19 pandemic. In our second section, we shift our focus to the strategies of resistance and escape by looking at how these strategies have gained relevance during the pandemic. Our critique of the prefigurative character of folk politics, as expressed in the strategies of resistance and escape, lead us to discuss more expansive strategies, particularly the strategy of eroding capitalism revisited from the lens of a revolutionary perspective. We discuss how this so-called "postcapitalist" strategy requires greater priority to anti-imperialism and the struggle against monopoly capitalism. In doing so, we also re-assert the centrality of the working class in today's politics.

Social Reform or Revolution, Revisited

Erik Olin Wright (2019: 80, 85) bases his arguments on a firm refusal of revolutionary politics. In his view, what he calls the strategy of "smashing capitalism" expresses the "classic strategic logic of revolutionaries" who led "the revolutionary tragedies of the twentieth century." He contends that revolutions — as an outcome of ruptural strategies — have failed to emancipate humanity, i.e., "eliminat[e] all forms of oppression" (8). We find this argument to be highly problematic for two main reasons. Today, the Cuban revolution is a model example that leads the way towards human emancipation. Not only is revolutionary Cuba designated as having "one of the world's most effective and unique" (Brouwer 2011; WHO 2008) healthcare systems and medical research infrastructure, but it has also "led to the world's largest conversion from conventional agriculture to organic and semi-organic agriculture" (Gürcan 2014: 131). It is "a world leader in hurricane preparedness and recovery" (Marcetic 2017) and ranked as one of the safest countries in terms of national and personal security (Petras and Veltmeyer 2009). Even the World Bank has labelled Cuba as a world leader in education (Bruns and Luque 2014). Cuba's historic achievements despite years of imperialist blockade alone testify to the emancipatory potential of revolutions. This emancipatory potential is also recognized by a majority of Russians who aspire to return to socialism thanks to the survived legacy of the Soviet revolution (teleSUR 2017; RT 2016).

A second reason why Wright's rejection of revolutions is highly problematic speaks to the necessity of acquiring state power for achieving substantial changes on the way towards human emancipation. While electoral success may serve as the first step towards acquiring state power, left-wing governments are doomed to fail if they cannot advance their electoral gains by expanding the dictatorship of the proletariat, where the means of production will be nationalized and socialized in strategic sectors such as energy, mining, infrastructure, transportation, communication, defence, medicine and healthcare, and education. The case of Latin America is highly instructive in this regard.

The 2000s witnessed a tremendous surge for Latin America's left-leaning social and political movements, which attained unparalleled strength and influence. This region-wide turn to the left was initiated by the rise to power of Hugo Chávez after the Venezuelan presidential election of 1998 (Gürcan 2019a). There followed the accession to office of left-leaning leaders in countries such as Chile, Brazil, Argentina, the Dominican Republic, Uruguay, Bolivia, Honduras, and Nicaragua (Gürcan 2019a). The Lula era in Brazil and that of Kirchners in Argentina were characterized by a multi-class alliance between the working masses and segments of the bourgeoisie represented by middle classes and so-called "national capitalists." The absence of a dictatorship of the proletariat and revolutionary measures to advance the gains of leftward policies resulted in Lula's imprisonment and the electoral failure of Cristina Kirchner, who was later indicted for corruption. In Argentina's case, for example, *kirchnerismo* lost its bourgeois support bases to the extent that it adopted a sharper political discourse in the face of the falling primary commodity prices and the persisting media power of the bourgeoise. Likewise, Venezuela has had to adopt more restrictive policies due to increasing US support for the bourgeois opposition and media under sanctions.

A similar situation would be expected in the case of a socialist electoral victory in the US. Would the American bourgeoisie and the US military-industrial complex, which happen to represent the vital interest of the world's largest companies, peacefully accept defeat or allow this socialist government to implement any radical policy? A frank answer will tell you that socialism cannot be peacefully built in the world's leading imperialist country unless a domestic revolution takes place or a series of wars and revolutions in the Global South paralyzes the US economy (and bourgeoisie) by disturbing the flow of imperialist rents. Nevertheless, the COVID-19 pandemic has done more than merely expose the impasse of capitalism. It has also debilitated governments and created a facilitative environment for the growth of revolutionary movements. In the meantime, the inability of capitalist reforms to bring about substantial changes adds much to the necessity of revolutions, as we discussed in the previous chapter.

A second strategy that Wright addresses is "dismantling capitalism." According to Wright, this strategy is adopted by those who bear socialist ideas and aspire to build socialism through peaceful means. In dismantling capitalism, the idea is to rely on state-directed reforms that facilitate a transition to democratic socialism. The transition period will be characterized by the development of a mixed economy where "there would be private capitalist banks alongside state-run banks; private capitalist firms alongside state enterprises, especially in transportation, utilities, health care, and certain branches of heavy industry" (2019: 87). In Wright's framework, this strategy leaves its place to a third called "taming capitalism," where social democratic governments look for solutions within capitalism by pursuing more moderate rather than socialist policies. Similar to Wright's portrayal of revolutions, this labelling is also highly problematic. It is not clear why Wright (2019: 79) failed to exclude the pro-capitalist strategy of "taming capitalism" from his categorization that he calls the "strategic logics" of "anticapitalist struggles." In any case, we have already addressed the option of "taming capitalism" in our previous chapter, since it has nothing to do with efforts at transcending capitalism. Certainly, the Great Reset and Green New Deal proposals can be easily associated with the strategy of "taming capitalism."

In the final analysis, it would be too early to conclude that revolutionary alternatives are outdated and no longer useful. Quite the contrary, the deepened crisis of global capitalism under the COVID-19 pandemic may well be creating an enabling environment conducive to revolutionary initiatives. Nonetheless, the pre-pandemic era already demonstrated how imperialism attempts to paralyze revolutionary governments in countries in the Global

South such as Cuba and Venezuela, both politically and economically, to disable fully democratic and peaceful means. This reveals the possibility of combining the strategies of smashing and dismantling capitalism, in varying degrees depending on the socioeconomic context at hand. As was discussed in our previous chapter, however, reformist strategies do not even have the potential to instigate either substantial or permanent changes.

Resistance and Escapism as Leftist Imaginaries

The strategy of "resisting capitalism" hinges upon forms of resistance such as protests, strikes, boycotts, and civil disobedience carried out with the aim of affecting the behaviour of capitalists and other dominant groups by exerting political pressure. Emblematic of those movements that employ the strategy of "resisting capitalism" are environmentalists protesting environmentally destructive behaviour, consumer movements boycotting corporations, and trade unions organizing strikes (Wright 2019). Unlike the strategy of "smashing capitalism," however, "resisting capitalism" restrains from capturing state power and tends to be more issue-based than the first three strategies, discussed in the previous section. This being said, the strategy of "resisting capitalism" bears a strong similarity to what Wright calls "escaping capitalism" as a fifth type of strategy for transcending capitalism. In this strategy, political actors restrain from engaging the state in fear of cooptation, driven by the belief that the state represents the most organized form of oppression and alienation. One could include in this category several escape attempts ranging from individualistic strategies such as the do-it-yourself movement and individual isolation ("get away from it all") to intentional communities such as cooperatives and ecological collectives as well as the sharing economy (e.g., peer-to-peer transactions, commons-based peer production, platform cooperatives, garden sharing, seed swaps, food banks, community kitchens, co-housing, time banking, bartering, open source software) (Wright 2019).

One should note that the COVID-19 pandemic period has triggered greater awareness of the solidarity economy. During the pandemic, the United Nations Inter-Agency Task Force on Social and Solidarity Economy (UNTFSSE) asserted that the pandemic has exposed the exclusionary and unsustainable character of the current development model (i.e., neoliberal capitalism). Against this backdrop, the UNTFSSE called for greater public support for the development of a "people-centred and planet-sensitive" model by taking advantage of the pandemic environment. According to the UNTFSSE, enterprises and organizations of the social and solidarity economy are the key actors in putting such a model into effect. UNTFSSE believes that there is a need to re-localize economies through cooperatives and community-based organizations amidst the dislocation of global value chains. These organizations allow for more inclusive and democratic governance in favour of the socioeconomically disadvantaged sectors of society in critical areas such as health, food, finance, education and training, culture, and aid (UNTFSSE 2020).

In a similar vein, the Intercontinental Network for the Promotion of Social Solidarity Economy urges extending local and national efforts at building the social and solidarity economy to a planetary level to build global solidarity networks and address the socioeconomic challenges of the pandemic (Ripess 2020). In the US, the Black Lives Matter (BLM) protests and democratic socialists have spurred a new wave of mutual aid collectives that even question capitalism, including the NYC-DSA Mutual Aid COVID-19 Relief Fund, the South Brooklyn Mutual Aid and Crown Heights Mutual Aid (Levin 2020). According to Trebor Scholz, a scholar-activist who is credited with coining the term "platform cooperativism," the COVID-19 pandemic provides a great opportunity for the expansion of platform cooperatives, i.e., cooperative "businesses that use a website, a mobile app, or protocol to sell goods or services" such as smart.coop, AgriHelp, Kolyma2, Deliveroo, CoopCycle, and Copyleft (Miller 2020; Schwertgen 2020; Calzada 2020).

Far from discouraging social mobilization, the COVID-19 pandemic has also brought the "resistance alternative" to the forefront of political struggles. Particularly, the year 2020 was marked by the Black Lives Matter movement, which is believed to be the largest social movement in American history. Triggered by the killing of Trayvon Martin as a result of police brutality in 2012, BLM protests have spread like wildfire. Police brutality against African Americans had triggered several other waves of protests by 2018. The year 2020 testified to the resurgence of the BLM movement following a series of police murders by May 2020, when mass protests erupted upon the killing of George Floyd. The estimated number of participants in this wave of protests in 2020 is 15 to 16 million, which elevated the BLM movement to the status of the largest movement in US history despite the COVID-19 conditions (Buchanan, Bui, and Patel 2020). These protests even led to the Strike for Black Lives, engaging thousands of workers in the US (Jacobson 2020). The BLM movement also voiced several radical and anti-systemic demands, such as defunding and disbanding the police, public housing, socialized healthcare, free education, and rent controls (Fattore and Gleeson 2020; Molyneux 2020; Thalen 2020). In June 2020, protesters went so far as to occupy the Capitol Hill neighbourhood of Seattle and declared the foundation of an autonomous zone (Bush 2020). The proclamation of this autonomous zone was accompanied by the creation of No Cop Co-op, which provided occupiers with free-of-charge food and health services. Occupiers also created a community garden and established a "Decolonization Conversation Café," which served as a public sphere for open political debates (Molyneux 2020; Burns and Keimig 2020; Burns 2020; Allam 2020). However, 2020's historic legacy of popular struggles was gravely overshadowed by right-wing anti-lockdown and pro-Trump protests, which culminated in right-wing groups storming the US Capitol building (Barrett, Raju, and Nickeas 2021; Martina, Renshaw, and Reid 2020; Wilson 2020).

Lately, the quick waning of popular protests and collective initiatives has led many to question the viability of the strategies of "resisting capitalism" and "escaping capitalism," labelled as "folk politics." Folk politics is often defined as "a constellation of ideas and intuitions within the contemporary left that informs the common-sense ways of organising, acting, and thinking politics" (Srnicek and Williams 2016: 28). Exemplary of folk politics are ethical consumerism such as the slow food movement, locavorism and the move-your-money movement, development microloans, credit unions, anarchist collectives, neighbourhood councils, cooperatives, recuperated workplaces, and protest movements (Srnicek and Williams 2016).

A common critique against folk politics is that it exerts a debilitating impact on the left because it prioritizes small-scale and localized forms of mobilization that are often driven by issue-based concerns expressed through fleeting actions such as "petitions, occupations, strikes, vanguard parties, affinity groups, and trade unions" (Srnicek and Williams 2016: 29). Folk politics — as embodied in what Wright (2019) calls the strategies of "resisting capitalism" and "escaping capitalism — is critiqued for ignoring long-term goals of mobilization while glorifying immediacy, spontaneity, and anti-authoritarianism (Srnicek and Williams 2016). This is also called "prefigurative politics," i.e., a political style that "practice[s] socialist principles in the present, not merely to imagine them for the future" (Downing 2001: 71). Horizontalism is a driving principle of prefigurative politics: it encourages the principles of self-management, direct democracy, inclusivity, and consensus-based decision-making. The prefigurative style of folk politics has the merit of mobilizing popular sectors against the hyper-individualization, hyper-competitiveness, and hyper-possessiveness of capitalism. However, they eventually fail to instigate significant changes in the status-quo (Sculos 2018; Srnicek and Williams 2016).

Neo-Zapatism is a prominent movement that symbolizes folk politics. Mexico's Zapatista struggle led by Ejército Zapatista de Liberación Nacional

(Zapatista Army of National Liberation, or EZLN) emerged in 1994 as the world's first major anti-neoliberal globalization struggle. It rose to prominence with mass protests and occupations of public buildings in reaction to Mexico's accession into the North American Free Trade Agreement (NAFTA). In line with the horizontalism of folk politics, it focused on strengthening civil society by pushing for bottom-up democratization (Gilbreth and Otero 2001; Hellman 1995). By advancing the autonomist slogan *"mandar obedeciendo"* (commanding by obeying), the EZLN formed "Juntas de Buen Gobierno" (Councils of Good Government) as autonomous local government bodies that "provide basic services in justice, health, education, land management, labour market, nutrition, commerce, information, culture, and local transport" (Benedikter 2014). Council members are elected for a three-year term and fulfill their duties on a weekly rotational basis. Membership is revocable by popular vote anytime (Rubin 2002; Harvey 1998; Gilbreth and Otero 2001).

Neo-Zapatismo inspired a new wave of anti-globalization activism worldwide (Gürcan 2019b); this eventually merged with massive anti-war protests in cities like Seattle, Prague, and London as well as at the World Social Forums, i.e., annual meetings of alter-globalist movements and organizations (Funke 2017). Despite the historic importance of neo-Zapatismo, however, the EZLN has suffered waning support and is now "permitted to exist in relative freedom simply because the state and capital do not see them as a threat" (Srnicek and Williams 2016: 86). Instead of growing into a revolutionary movement that could expand to the rest of the country through stronger alliances, the EZLN has fetishized prefigurative politics and horizontalism, which ultimately proved to be "a serious liability" (86).

After the 1990s, the crisis of global capitalism resulted in another wave of global protests, in which economic demands and working-class issues were strongly represented. The period of 2010–11 marked the breaking point of this new wave of popular contention. Worthy of note in this connection is the outbreak of the Arab Spring in 2010 and how it inspired global occupation movements, starting with Occupy Wall Street, Europe's anti-austerity campaigns, and other disruptive movements, such as France's Yellow Vests in the period 2018–20 (Gürcan 2019b). According to Nick Srnicek and Alex Williams, such movements represent the folk politics tradition, albeit in varying degrees. Their main failure lies in the inability to forge an expansive left "aiming to transform capitalism in fundamental ways" (Srnicek and Williams 2016: 89), despite their crucial contribution to long-term change in values and attitudes.

In the case of the Arab Spring, this movement is considered the largest social mobilization in the Middle East since the collapse of the Soviet Union. Its historic importance also stems from the fact that it catalyzed the outbreak of a new wave of popular contention in the context of the crisis of global capitalism (Gürcan 2019b). In December 2010, Tunisian working-class and civic organizations massed after the self-immolation of a street vendor who had been repressed by police forces. Social mobilization was so vigorous and united in its aims that after three weeks, the president was forced to resign. Inspired by this success, similar mobilizations began in Egypt, Libya, Syria, and elsewhere. Eventually, however, the Arab Spring turned into an Arab Winter. In Egypt, with considerable popular support, the July 2013 coup d'état restored military rule. Eventually, Egyptians and Tunisians failed to sustain an expansive movement that aims at the dismantling of capitalism. Under Western intervention, moreover, Libya became mired in a civil war that has produced tens of thousands of casualties. Many Western-backed mercenaries in Libya would eventually move on to the Syria campaign. Thanks to continued Western support, Syria became the centre stage of one of the world's largest humanitarian crises since the Second World War (Otero and Gürcan 2016; Gürcan 2019b).

The Arab Spring had a global influence: it also struck a chord in Europe. Therefore, it is relevant to address the economic-structural context of Europe's anti-austerity protests in several countries, such as Italy, Portugal, Spain, Greece, and Britain. One of the immediate manifestations of the European crisis was the decline and disappearance of economic growth, accompanied by rising unemployment levels (Gürcan 2019a). However, despite widespread street protests, strikes and picket lines, "the moves necessary to transform the social fabric were never taken" (Srnicek and Williams 2016: 84). Perhaps with the exception of the Podemos, a Spanish movement party that was created following anti-austerity protests and joined the coalition government in 2020, the main liability of anti-austerity movements is that they have failed to transcend their initial form as protest movements.

The US occupation movement drew strong inspiration from both the Arab Spring and European anti-austerity movements. The US economic crisis of 2007–08 started with the explosion of the subprime bubble (Gürcan 2019b). This crisis had a deep symbolic impact on US society, given that homeownership was among the most important attractions of the so-called American Dream (Ross 2016). The crisis, therefore, produced widespread disillusionment by dissipating aspirations for a middle-class lifestyle. Moreover, the bursting of the subprime bubble also affected the real economy and culminated in one of the worst economic crises in US history. Important consequences included increased rates of unemployment and homelessness, which eventually triggered US occupation movements in 2011 (Ross 2016).

The Occupy movement, which erupted in September 2011 and soon grew into a global protest movement that involved over 2000 cities worldwide, is a case in point regarding the loss of popular confidence in neoliberal capitalism, especially since this movement brought socialistic demands to the mainstream of society for the first time since the 1970s (Chomsky 2012: 41, electronic copy). The Occupy movement testified to the insurgence of what came to be called the precariat, a working-class stratum "who live a precarious existence," emblematized in the slogan "We are the 99%" (Chomsky 2012: 24). The 1% were associated with financial institutions such as Bank of America, CitiBank, JP Morgan, and Wells Fargo. Occupiers thus came forward with radical proposals for the abolition of the legal personhood of corporations and the end of corporate control over the US political system. Similar to neo-Zapatismo, alter-globalizers, the Arab Spring, and anti-austerity movements, the Occupy movement assumes historic importance for its inspirational value. This being said, Occupy's influence has gradually waned due to several shortcomings related to folk politics. Occupy adopted a prefigurative approach, where dominant tactics such as protesting, marching, and occupying assumed a ritualistic character. Occupied public spaces served as the movement' headquarters, and these headquarters were later rendered dysfunctional in the absence of occupied public spaces. Overall, the Occupy movement ended up fetishizing horizontalism and insisting on consensus decision-making in general assemblies, which eventually served to paralyze its decisional structure. The movement also refrained from formulating concrete demands to prevent internal divisions. At the end of the day, these limitations call for a more expansive approach to transcending capitalism (Srnicek and Williams 2016).

One could easily observe that COVID-19 conditions such as wearing masks, keeping social distance, and health-related fears have not sufficed to discourage social protests. On the contrary, the pandemic has witnessed high levels of social mobilization and brought to the forefront the strategy of resistance. Notably, the year of the pandemic was centrestage to one of the most intense waves of civil rights protests in US history. However, these protests were met with widescale anti-lockdown protests and pro-Trump demonstrations representing the far-right. Yet, the pandemic seems to have aroused some degree of awareness about the effectiveness of the social solidarity economy. This being said, this awareness has so far failed to transcend its embryonic phase and has proved to be ineffective in transforming capitalism in the absence of a revolutionary government to provide substantial support for popular alternatives. One could argue that the local and isolated character of these developments are a defining feature of folk politics, which points to the need for more expansive strategies, as we discuss in the next section.

Eroding Capitalism, But How?
A Critical Perspective into Postcapitalism

The sixth and final strategy in Erik Olin Wright's (2019) classification is the strategy of "eroding capitalism," which also responds to the need to develop a more expansive approach than the prefigurative approach of folk politics embodied in the strategies of resisting and escaping capitalism. In Wright's categorization, eroding capitalism reflects a strategic vision that combines the prefigurative approach of resistance and collective escape with the state-led strategy of dismantling capitalism. From a realistic perspective, however, putting the radicalism of resistance and the utopianism of collective escape into practice requires the conquest of state power and harsher measures to prevent bourgeois resistance. Therefore, the strategy of eroding capitalism would be incomplete without incorporating elements from the revolutionary strategy of smashing capitalism.

What the strategy of eroding capitalism really envisions to achieve is the creation of a "postcapitalist society." It is possible to describe postcapitalism as the outcome of a "transitional program" to build socialism, which "expand[s] postmarket institutions and practices within capitalism" (Mason 2020: 292). Abolishing such a complicated socioeconomic system as capitalism is a long and complicated process rather than a one-day job. Therefore, the idea here is to gradually "create non-market units within a market economy" (Mason 2020: 287) through the mobilization of solidarity economy movements and the expansion of public services under a revolutionary government. In this project, the revolutionary government will assume a minimum of five basic tasks: the suppression of monopoly capitalists; the creation of universal basic services; the promotion of solidarity economy and collaborative business models; paying everyone a basic income; and the management of information as a public good (Mason 2020, 2016).

The first task concerns monopoly capitalism, which can be understood as a capitalist system dominated by giant (i.e., highly bureaucratized, hierarchical, management-controlled and financially independent) corporations and strong imperialist states that further the interests of giant corporations (Baran and Sweezy 1966). The neoliberal era has contributed to nothing but the expansion of monopoly capitalism at unprecedented levels. With the advent of technology, therefore, our societies are faced with a rapidly intensifying contradiction "between the possibility of free, abundant socially produced goods, and a system of monopolies, banks and governments struggling to maintain control over power and information" (Mason 2016: 291). Given the centrality of this contradiction, perhaps the first step in the implementation of postcapitalism would be to suppress and socialize monopolies under revolutionary governments, especially those dominating the information and communications technology industries, considering the increased eminence of digital capitalism.

Second, revolutionary governments should redeploy state power to establish universal basic services, especially in critical areas of social reproduction such as healthcare, daycare, education, and housing. This would in turn reverse neoliberal welfare policies driven by market-oriented, conditional, and short-term approaches that help nothing but to reproduce and deepen inequalities. Third, revolutionary governments should encourage bottom-up initiatives (e.g., consumer and producer cooperatives, platform cooperatives and peer-to-peer collaborative production, housing cooperatives and co-housing practices, credit unions, small producers) based on the principle of economic democracy (Wright 2019). In this regard, public programs can be deployed to assist the conversion of capitalist firms, whilst public credit institutions can provide the necessary financial environment facilitating the creation and sustenance of economic solidarity initiatives. In the meantime, publicly funded training programs will be able to develop skills for cooperative management (Wright 2019).

Fourth, the postcapitalist project will enable revolutionary governments to pay everyone a basic income to support the free expansion of solidarity economies. This "would reduce the dependency of worker-owners on market income generated by the cooperative enterprise and thus reduce the risks of forming a cooperative" (Wright 2019: 147). Fifth, and finally, the rise of information-rich economies under digital capitalism has greatly expanded the socialized nature of production: "With purely physical goods, consumption by one person generally blocks their use by another: it's my cigarette, not yours, my hire car, my cappuccino, my half-hour of psychotherapy. Not yours. But with an mp3 track, the information is the commodity. It can technically exist in many physical forms" (Mason 2016: 242). In other words, the supply of information is nowadays close to infinite. Under these conditions, the sustenance of capitalism depends on the power of monopolies to prevent the spontaneous emergence of zero-cost products through rent-seeking behaviour and a firmer property rights regime (Mason 2016). With this in mind, revolutionary governments should not only suppress monopolies; they should also turn information into a public good by restricting the intellectual property rights regime and encouraging open access.

Our own understanding of postcapitalism as the desired outcome acquired by a strategy of "eroding capitalism" differs from the commonly accepted definitions of postcapitalism. For one thing, we reject the techno-determinist argument that "postcapitalism is possible because of [the] impact of the new technology" (Mason 2016: 18). Instead, postcapitalism as a transitional program has more to do with the concrete ability of revolutionary governments to capture state power and control the means of production in strategic sectors by starting with the nationalization or socialization of monopolies, which is only possible under the conditions of the dictatorship of the proletariat. Socialized state capitalism that aspires to build higher (and more democratic) forms of socialism under the guidance of a revolutionary government has always been a possible alternative, even before the Fourth Industrial Revolution. This being said, there is no question that revolutionary governments must give due attention to the efficient use and democratization of information technologies as a strategic component of productive forces under digital capitalism.

The dominant understanding conceives postcapitalism as the realization of a post-work society and universal emancipation where "the law of value ceases to operate" (Mason 2020: 292). Indeed, revolutionary governments aspiring to a higher form of socialism and the creation of communist society would be driven by a vision to abolish the capitalist law of value. However, postcapitalism — understood as a transitional program — will only mark the first step towards socialism. One should note that there are more immediate challenges and threats to the realization of postcapitalism, namely the persisting existence of imperialism. In a world system dominated by monopoly-capitalist imperialism, revolutionary governments in the Global South will not be able to satisfy their basic demands and achieve the standards of the Third Industrial Revolution, let alone those of the Fourth Industrial Revolution. How can one expect countries such as Cuba and Venezuela to realize Paul Mason's postcapitalist techno-utopia faced with Western-imperialist military aggression and meddling with elections? It follows that both revolutions and anti-imperialism are a priority for postcapitalism, given that there can be no postcapitalist project without revolutionary governments and a strong anti-imperialist front worldwide.

Our conceptualization of postcapitalism also diverges from the dominant understanding of postcapitalism when it comes to the working class.

The dominant postcapitalist view on the working class finds its expression in Paul Mason's argument that it has "become impossible to imagine [the] working class ... overthrowing capitalism" (2016: 352). On the contrary, there is ample evidence that the working class still resides at the forefront of world-historical struggles challenging global capitalism. For example, the working class had significant weight in the rise of Latin America's leftist governments (Gürcan and Mete 2017). A case in point is Luiz Inácio Lula da Silva, Brazil's former president (2003–11), who was a former union leader who took part in the foundation of the Workers' Party (WP). The origins of the WP go back to the strikes at the Scania plant in São Paulo's ABC region in 1978–79, and trade unions constituted the core of the WP's popular base of support (Baiocchi 2004; Samuels 2004; Gürcan and Mete 2017). The labour movement played a no less significant role in the ascendancy of the Argentine left after the 2001 economic crisis, as a result of which hundreds of thousands of workers took to the streets and called for a rollback of neoliberal policies. Not surprisingly, traditionally strong trade unions, alongside the proponents of social-movement unionism in the informal and unemployed sectors, took the lead in the protests and served as a strategic popular base of the Kirchner governments (2003–15) (Onuch 2014; Wylde 2011; Gürcan and Mete 2017). Likewise, the Movimiento al Socialismo (MAS), Bolivia's governing left party, can be seen as a "trade union initiative," whose core leadership is represented by the coca leaf growers' unions, in alliance with other labour unions and social movements (Tapia 2008; Gürcan and Mete 2017).

The case of the Arab Spring is similarly instructive as regards the increasing relevance of the working class (Gürcan 2019b). The Arab Spring cannot be reduced to a mere set of anti-authoritarian struggles, not only because the working class and its economic demands played a key role, but also thanks to how these struggles exerted a huge influence on occupation and anti-austerity movements worldwide (Della Porta 2015; Kousis 2016; Gürcan and Mete 2017). Perhaps most importantly, the Arab Spring came to be associated with the slogan "Bread, Dignity, Freedom." It is significant that "bread" comes first in this slogan — a class-based demand. Meanwhile, the Tunisian General Labour Union (Union Générale Tunisienne du Travail, UGTT) took the lead in the Arab Spring protests, mainly thanks to its nation-wide network and its strong tradition of struggle. UGTT had also played an important role in Tunisia's independence (Hechiche 2017; Weipert-Fenner 2018; O'Brien 2015). The relatively democratic outcome of Tunisia's Arab Spring can even be associated with the relatively strong participation and autonomy of Tunisia's working-class movement. In Tunisia, the working-class movement reacted to the negative implications of privatization and liberalization (Allinson 2015).

In fact, the Arab Spring in both Tunisia and Egypt can be seen as an outcome of neoliberalism (Hinnebusch 2018). Besides UGTT, unemployed university graduates and youth assumed key roles, also thanks to their experience accumulated from the post-2006 period. At this time, the Union of Unemployed Graduates (Union des diplômés chômeurs, UDC) started to mobilize against irregular privatizations and arbitrary hiring standards. UDC made its name heard in 2008 during the Gafsa mining basin protests against layoffs and subcontracting. These lasted for six months, during which the UDC leadership was instrumental in uniting unemployed and subcontracted workers, high-school students, and working-class families. They constituted one of Tunisia's largest social mobilizations before the Arab Spring and were seen as an antecedent of the Arab Spring itself (Weipert-Fenner and Wolff 2016; Weipert-Fenner 2018; Gobe 2010).

One should also point to the key role of the working class in Europe's anti-austerity protests (Gürcan 2019b). Italy experienced one of the earliest experiments in class-based struggles during the crisis of neoliberal capitalism. In fact, the Italian experiment preceded even the Arab Spring conjuncture. In the 2009–14 period alone, trade unions participated in almost half of all the anti-austerity protests that took place in Italy. Furthermore, the protesters, nearly 70% of whom were estimated to be working class, brought to the forefront class-based slogans about justice and democracy, targeting the EU's top-down austerity policies. Budget cuts, privatizations, and the deterioration of public services induced a massive reaction on the part of the Italian working class (Andretta 2017).

Insurance and wage cuts, tax hikes, and public service cuts, which have been imposed by the EU since 2010, triggered massive street protests. Trade unions took the lead in these protests. Interestingly, for example, Portugal had experienced only five general strikes between 1974 and 2009. However, the general strikes in the 2010–14 period almost equalled that number. Trade unions also took part in marches and demonstrations, whose underlying slogans included "Jobs, Health, and Education! Not Troika!" (Fernandes 2017).

Spain's anti-austerity protests were initiated in 2010 against the backdrop of union calls for a general strike. The year 2011 was marked by a students' strike against budget cuts in education and high tuition fees. A platform called Juventud Sin Futuro (Youth Without a Future) organized mass protests with the slogan "Homeless, Jobless, Pensionless, Fearless." Together with a grassroots citizens' network called Real Democracy NOW!, the actions of Juventud Sin Futuro gave birth to the Indignados movement, which organized massive protests in May 2011, gathering tens of thousands of participants. Like the Arab Spring, these protests served as an immense source of inspiration for US occupation movements and other anti-austerity movements in Europe (Perugorría, Shalev, and Tejerina 2016; Gürcan 2019b). Indignados' underlying demands included such class-based and distributive matters as controlling the banks, the right to housing, fighting unemployment, and the improvement of social services and democracy. Even though Indignados were critical of traditional unions' ambivalence towards the government, active union mobilization served as a key trigger in the emergence and escalation of anti-austerity protests. Moreover, social-movement unionism actively participated in Spain's anti-austerity movement (Romanos 2017).

Greece was perhaps the place where working-class demands were raised most strongly (Gürcan 2019b). It was at the forefront of anti-austerity protests, as shown by the fact that in 2010–13 alone, the country witnessed at least 27 general strikes, along with other anti-austerity movements in which the working class participated. Moreover, the largest protests in this period were those that involved the working class. The protests reached their peak on June 28–29, 2011, when Greece was undergoing a general strike; 800 protesters were injured due to police repression (Dufour, Nez, and Ancelovici 2016; Della Porta 2015; Kriesi 2016; Vogiatzoglou 2017).

To conclude this final section, a critical evaluation of past attempts at disturbing and transcending capitalism reveals that the post-COVID era requires more expansive strategies that can successfully combine revolutionary and state-driven initiatives with bottom-up alternatives. This is essential for achieving substantial gains in transcending capitalism. In the meantime, we critically revisited the postcapitalist strategy of eroding capitalism by drawing attention to the persisting centrality of the working class. Our critical, but sympathetic appraisal also exposed traces of techno-determinism and the lack of engagement with the phenomenon of imperialism in postcapitalist thinking. Instead, we proposed a more modest conceptualization for the postcapitalist strategy of eroding capitalism as a transitional program and first step towards human emancipation.

Review and Discussion

In this chapter, we discussed viable alternatives to capitalist reformism for the post-COVID era. Our discussion drew on a critical synthesis of postcapitalist thinking and Erik Olin Wright's (2019) classification of essential left-wing strategies to transcend capitalism from a revolutionary and anti-imperialist perspective. From this synthesis, we extracted an expansive and long-term strategy that may succeed in combining revolutionary and state-led strategies with a social-economy approach: the postcapitalist strategy of eroding capitalism as a minimum program of achievable demands towards universal emancipation. While past attempts at challenging capitalism demonstrate the increasing relevance of the working class, the deepening crisis of capitalism leads to new revolutionary prospects with some dose of Jacobinism and economic democracy. The COVID-period in 2020–21 has already created fertile ground for massive protests and the solidarity economy, which can be taken to a higher level with the successful implementation of a revolutionary project that transcends the confines of bourgeois democracy.

We identify two key challenges to the revolutionary program of postcapitalism: monopoly capitalism and imperialism. A notable and perhaps the most immediate target of postcapitalism is monopoly capitalism. Without suppressing and expropriating monopolies, a revolutionary government cannot render the solidarity economy a dominant institution alongside the public sector. Similarly, the imperialist system is wired to suffocate every revolutionary initiative to render the solidarity economy and public sector dominant institutions. As far as revolutionary governments in the Global South are concerned, imperialist countries will continue to meddle in elections, provide support for bourgeois political actors seeking to sabotage the economy through various means, lead foreign military interventions, and impose an endless number of sanctions. The strong imperialist interests represented by the political elites of advanced capitalist countries will not peacefully allow the rise to power of a truly socialist government nor the implementation of a truly postcapitalist project in their own countries.

REFERENCES

Allam, H. 2020. "'Remember Who We're Fighting For': The Uneasy Existence of Seattle's Protest Camp." *NPR*, June 18. <https://www.npr.org/2020/06/17/879041066/seattle-strangers-discuss-racial-injustice-while-protesting>.

Allinson, J. 2015. "Class Forces, Transition and the Arab Uprisings: A Comparison of Tunisia, Egypt and Syria." *Democratization* 22, 2: 294–314.

Andretta, M. 2017. Neoliberalism and Its Discontents in Italy: Protests Without Movement? In D.D. Porta, M. Andretta, T. Fernandes, F. O'Connor, E. Romanos, and M. Vogiatzoglou (eds.), *Neoliberalism and its Discontents in the Economic Crisis* (pp. 201–224). London: Palgrave Macmillan.

Baiocchi, G. 2004. "The Party and the Multitude: Brazil's Workers' Party (PT) and the Challenges of Building a Just Social Order in A Globalizing Context." *Journal of World-Systems Research* 10, 1: 199–215.

Baran, P.A., and P. Sweezy. 1966. *Monopoly Capital.* New York: Monthly Review Press.

Barrett, T., M. Raju, and P. Nickeas. 2021. "US Capitol Secured, 4 Dead after Rioters Stormed the Halls of Congress to Block Biden's Win." CNN, January 7. <https://edition.cnn.com/2021/01/06/politics/us-capitol-lockdown/index.html>.

Benedikter, T. 2014. "The Caracoles de Chiapas (Mexico): 20 Years of Zapatista Struggle — 10 Years of Self-Organized Autonomy." *Infowelat,* April 28. <http://infowelat.com/the-caracoles-de-chiapas-mexico-20-years-of-zapatista-struggle-10-years-of-self-organized-autonomy.html>.

Brouwer, S. 2011. *Revolutionary Doctors: How Venezuela and Cuba Are Changing the World's Conception of Health Care.* New York: NYU Press.

Bruns, B., and J. Luque. 2014. "Great Teachers: How to Raise Student Learning in Latin America and the Caribbean." *World Bank.* <https://www.worldbank.org/content/dam/Worldbank/document/LAC/Great_Teachers-How_to_Raise_Student_Learning-Barbara-Bruns-Advance%20Edition.pdf>.

Buchanan, L., Q. Bui, and J. Patel. 2020. "Black Lives Matter May Be the Largest Movement in U.S. History." *The New York Times,* July 3. <https://www.nytimes.com/interactive/2020/07/03/us/george-floyd-protests-crowd-size.html>.

Burns, C. 2020. "The Capitol Hill Autonomous Zone Renames, Expands, and Adds Film Programming." *The Stranger,* June 10. <https://www.thestranger.com/slog/2020/06/10/43880223/the-capitol-hill-autonomous-zone-renames-expands-and-adds-film-programming>.

Burns, C., and J. Keimig. 2020. "Slog PM: Juneteenth Freedom Marches, Mayor Durkan Meets Mayor Teargas, Yakima Overwhelmed by COVID-19." *The Stranger,* June 19. <https://www.thestranger.com/slog/2020/06/19/43938194/slog-pm-juneteenth-freedom-marches-mayor-durkan-meets-mayor-teargas-yakima-overwhelmed-by-covid-19>.

Bush, E. 2020. "Welcome to the Capitol Hill Autonomous Zone, Where Seattle Protesters Gather Without Police." *Seattle Time,* August 12. <https://www.seattletimes.com/seattle-news/welcome-to-the-capitol-hill-autonomous-zone-where-seattle-protesters-gather-without-police/>.

Calzada, I. 2020. "Platform and Data Co-operatives amidst European Pandemic Citizenship." *Sustainability* 12, 20: 8309.

Chomsky, N. 2012. *Occupy.* UK: Penguin Books.

Della Porta, D. 2015. *Social Movements in Times of Austerity: Bringing Capitalism Back into Protest Analysis.* Cambridge/Malden: Polity Press.

Downing, J. 2001) *Radical Media: Rebellious Communication and Social Movements.* Thousand Oaks, CA: Sage.

Dufour, P., H. Nez, and M. Ancelovici. 2016. "From the Indignados to Occupy: Prospects for Comparison." In M. Ancelovici, P. Dufour and H. Nez (eds.), *Street Politics in the Age of Austerity: From the Indignados to Occupy* (pp. 11–42). Amsterdam: Amsterdam University Press.

Fattore, T., and K. Gleeson. 2020. "Guest Editors' Introduction: State Violence—

Practices and Responses." *International Journal of Crime, Justice and Social Democracy* 9, 4: i–vi.

Fernandes, T. 2017. "Late Neoliberalism and Its Discontents: The Case of Portugal." In D.D. Porta, M. Andretta, T. Fernandes, F. O'Connor, E. Romanos and M. Vogiatzoglou (eds.), *Neoliberalism and Its Discontents in the Economic Crisis* (pp.169–200). London: Palgrave Macmillan.

Funke, P.N. 2017. "The Global Social Justice Movement and its Subterranean Afterlife in Europe—the Rhizomatic Epoch of Contention—from Zapatistas to the European Anti-Austerity Protests." In H.E. Vanden, P.N. Funke, and G. Prevost (eds.), *The New Global Politics: Global Social Movements in the Twenty-First Century (Rethinking Globalizations* (pp. 174–189). Abington: Routledge.

Gilbreth, C., and G. Otero. 2001. "Democratization in Mexico: The Zapatista Uprising and Civil Society." *Latin American Perspectives* 28, 7: 7–29.

Gobe, E. 2010. "The Gafsa Mining Basin between Riots and a Social Movement: Meaning and Significance of a Protest Movement in Ben Ali's Tunisia." *Sciences de l'Homme et de la Société* 1: 1–21.

Gürcan, E.C. 2014. "Cuban Agriculture and Food Sovereignty: Beyond Civil-Society-Centric and Globalist Paradigms." *Latin American Perspectives* 41, 4: 129–146.

____. 2019a. *Multipolarization, South-South Cooperation and the Rise of Post-Hegemonic Governance*. Abington: Routledge.

____. 2019b. "Küresel Kapitalizmin Krizi, Sınıflar ve 'Yeni' Toplumsal Hareketler [The Crisis of Global Capitalism, Social Classes, and "New" Social Movements]." *Praksis* 50, 2: 71–94.

Gürcan, E.C., and B. Mete. 2017. *Neoliberalism and the Changing Face of Unionism: The Combined and Uneven Development of Class Capacities in Turkey*. New York: Palgrave.

Harvey, N. 1998. *The Chiapas Rebellion: The Struggle for Land and Liberty*. Durham: Duke University Press.

Healy, S., B. Chitranshi, G. Diprose, et al. 2020. "Planetary Food Commons and Postcapitalist Post-COVID Food Futures." *Development* (online published). <doi: 10.1057/s41301-020-00267-9>.

Hechiche, A.H. 2017. "The Role of Social Movements in Tunisia's Jasmine Revolution." In H.E. Vanden, P.N. Funke and G. Prevost (eds.), *The New Global Politics: Global Social Movements in the Twenty-First Century (Rethinking Globalizations)* (pp. 94–110). Abington: Routledge.

Hellman, J.A. 1995. "The Riddle of New Social Movements: Who They Are and What They Do." In S. Halebsky and R.L. Harris (eds.), *Capital, Power, and Inequality in Latin America* (pp. 65–183). Boulder: Westview.

Hinnebusch, R. 2018. "Understanding Regime Divergence in the Post-Uprising Arab States." *Journal of Historical Sociology* 31, 1: 39–52.

Jacobson, D. 2020. "National 'Strike for Black Lives' to Fight Racism, Low Wages." *UPI*, July 20. <https://www.upi.com/Top_News/US/2020/07/20/National-Strike-for-Black-Lives-to-fight-racism-low-wages/7281595239459/>.

Kousis, M. 2016. "The Spatial Dimensions of the Greek Protest Campaign Against the Troika's Memoranda and Austerity, 2010–2013." In M. Ancelovici, P. Dufour and H. Nez (eds.), *Street Politics in the Age of Austerity: From the Indignados to*

Occupy (pp. 147–174), Amsterdam: Amsterdam University Press.

Kriesi, N. 2016. "Mobilization of Protest in the Age of Austerity." In M. Ancelovici, P. Dufour and H. Nez (eds.), *Street Politics in the Age of Austerity: From the Indignados to Occupy* (pp. 67–90). Amsterdam: Amsterdam University Press.

Levin, A. 2020. "Rebuilding the Solidarity Economy During COVID-19." *The Progressive*, December 11. <https://progressive.org/dispatches/solidarity-economy-during-covid-levin-201211/>.

Marcetic, B. 2017. "Before the Hurricane." *Jacobin*, April 30. <https://jacobinmag.com/2017/08/hurricane-harvey-cuba-disaster-plan>.

Martina, M., J. Renshaw, and T. Reid. 2020. "How Trump Allies Have Organized and Promoted Anti-Lockdown Protests." *Reuters*, April 22. <https://www.reuters.com/article/us-health-coronavirus-trump-protests-idUSKCN2233ES>.

Mason, P. 2016. *PostCapitalism: A Guide to Our Future*. UK: Penguin Books.

____. 2020. "The Postcapitalist Transition: Policy Implications for the Left." *The Political Quarterly* 91, 2: 287–298.

Miller, V. 2020. "Cooperatives Reloaded. Let's Own the Digital World!" *Eurac Research*, September 9. <https://beta.eurac.edu/en/blogs/covid-19/cooperatives-reloaded-lets-own-the-digital-world>.

Molyneux, J. 2020. "The Great Rebellion." *Irish Marxist Review* 9, 27: 6–11.

Nelson, A. 2020. "COVID-19: Capitalist and Postcapitalist Perspectives." *Human Geography* 13, 3: 305–309.

O'Brien, T. 2015. "The Primacy of Political Security: Contentious Politics and Insecurity in the Tunisian Revolution." *Democratization* 22, 7: 1209–1229.

Onuch, O. 2014. "It's the Economy, Stupid," or Is It? The Role of Political Crisis in Mass Mobilization: The Case of Argentina in 2001." In C. Levey, D. Ozarow, and C. Wylde (eds.), *Argentina Since the 2001 Crisis: Recovering the Past, Reclaiming the Future* (pp. 89–114). New York: Palgrave Macmillan.

Otero, G., and E.C. Gürcan. 2016. "The Arab Spring and the Syrian Refugee Crisis." *The Monitor*, Canadian Center for Policy Alternatives 22, 5: 16–17.

Perugorría, I., M. Shalev, and B. Tejerina. 2016. "The Spanish Indignados and Israel's Social Judgement Movement." In M. Ancelovici, P. Dufour and H. Nez (eds.), *Street Politics in the Age of Austerity: From the Indignados to Occupy* (pp. 91–120). Amsterdam: Amsterdam University Press.

Petras, J. and H. Veltmeyer. 2009. *What's Left in Latin America? Regime Change in New Times*, first ed. Abington: Routledge.

Ripess. 2020. "COVID-19: Globalising Solidarity Is the Response We Need Now! *Ripess*. <http://www.ripess.org/covid-19-globalising-solidarity-is-the-response-we-need-now/?lang=en>.

Romanos, E. 2017. "Late Neoliberalism and Its Indignados: Contention in Austerity Spain." In D.D. Porta, M. Andretta, T. Fernandes, et al. (eds.), *Neoliberalism and its Discontents in the Economic Crisis* (pp. 131–167). London: Palgrave Macmillan.

Ross, G. 2016. "Austerity and New Spaces for Protest: The Financial Crisis and Its Victims." In M. Ancelovici, P. Dufour and H. Nez (eds.), *Street Politics in the Age of Austerity: From the Indignados to Occupy* (pp. 43–66). Amsterdam: Amsterdam University Press. <https://doi.org/10.1515/9789048525461-003>.

RT. 2016. "Most Russians Regret USSR Collapse, Dream of Its Return, Poll Shows."

RT, April 19. <https://www.rt.com/russia/340158-most-russians-regret-ussr-has/>.

Rubin, J. 2002. "From Che to Marcos: The Changing Grassroots in Latin America." *Dissent* 49, 3: 39–47.

Samuels, D. 2004. "From Socialism to Social Democracy: Party Organization and the Transformation of the Workers' Party in Brazil." *Comparative Political Studies* 37, 9: 999–1024.

Schwertgen, D. 2020. "Platform Cooperatives: Workplace Democracy for the 21st Century?" DIEM25, July 18. <https://diem25.org/platform-cooperatives-workplace-democracy-for-the-21st-century/>.

Sculos, B. 2018. "Minding the Gap: Marxian Reflections on the Transition from Capitalism to Postcapitalism." *triple* 16, 2: 676–686.

Srnicek, N., and A. Williams. 2016. *Inventing the Future: Postcapitalism and a World Without Work*. London and New York: Verso Book.

Tapia, L. 2008. "Bolivia: The Left and the Social Movements." In P. Barrett, D. Chavez, and C. Rodríguez-Garavito (eds.), *The New Latin American Left: Utopia Reborn* (pp. 215–231). London: Pluto Press.

teleSUR. 2017. "Most Russians Prefer Return of Soviet Union and Socialism: Poll." *teleSUR*, August 19. <https://www.telesurenglish.net/news/Poll-Most-Russians-Prefer-Return-of-Soviet-Union-and-Socialism-20160420-0051.html>.

Thalen, M. 2020. "Seattle's 'Autonomous Zone' Releases List of Demands." *Daily Dot*, June 10. <https://www.dailydot.com/debug/seattle-capitol-hill-autonomous-zone-demands/>.

UNTFSSE. 2020. "What Role for the Social and Solidarity Economy in the Post COVID-19 Crisis Recovery?" ILO, June <https://www.ilo.org/wcmsp5/groups/public/---ed_emp/---emp_ent/---coop/documents/publication/wcms_748794.pdf>.

Varoufakis, Y. 2020. "The Post-Capitalist Hit of the Summer." *Common Dreams*, August 31. <https://www.commondreams.org/views/2020/08/31/post-capitalist-hit-summer>.

Vogiatzoglou, M. 2017. "Turbulent Flow: Anti-Austerity Mobilization in Greece." In D. Della Porta, D. Romanos, F. O'Connor, et al. (eds.), *Late Neoliberalism and Its Discontents in the Economic Crisis: Comparing Social Movements in the European Periphery* (pp. 99–129). Cham, Switzerland: Palgrave Macmillan.

Weipert-Fenner, I. 2018. "Unemployed Mobilisation in Times of Democratisation: The Union of Unemployed Graduates in post-Ben Ali Tunisia." *The Journal of North African Studies* (online published). <doi: 10.1080/13629387.2018.1535317>.

Weipert-Fenner, I., and J. Wolff. 2016. "Unemployed Movements in the Global South: The Cases of Argentina and Tunisia." *Peace Research Institute Frankfurt* 32: 1–19.

WHO. 2008. "Cuba's Primary Health Care Revolution: 30 Years On." <https://www.who.int/bulletin/volumes/86/5/08-030508/en/>.

Wilson, J. 2020. "The Rightwing Groups Behind Wave of Protests Against Covid-19 Restrictions." *The Guardian*, April 17. <https://www.theguardian.com/world/2020/apr/17/far-right-coronavirus-protests-restrictions>.

Wright, E.O. 2010. *Envisioning Real Utopias*. London and New York: Verso Book.
____. 2019. *How to Be an Anticapitalist in the Twenty-First Century*. London and New York: Verso Book.
Wylde, C. 2011. "State, Society and Markets in Argentina: The Political Economy of Neodesarrollismo under Néstor Kirchner, 2003–2007." *Bulletin of Latin American Research* 30, 4: 436–452.

Conclusion

The development of humanity has reached a stage where the expansion of its productive forces — a society's ability to create material values — makes it possible to eradicate hunger, poverty, and war. Resolving such issues is no longer a matter of scarcity (nor climate change or eradicating resources) but rather disorganization of our relations of production, understood as the totality of our social relations governing production, distribution, consumption, and ownership. Marxism suggests that the main contradiction of capitalism occurs between the social character of the productive forces and the private character of the relations of production. On the one hand, economic activity — as the material basis for the reproduction and development of society — entails large and complex production systems operating on a global scale (Harnecker 1976). The social character of productive forces finds perhaps its sharpest expression in "increasing interdependence among all branches of production, between industry and education, between capitalist management and the flow of information, and between the economy and the state" (Jessop 1986: 56). On the other hand, the capitalist relations of production organize economic activity in an "anarchic, uncoordinated manner determined by the private interests of individual capitalists concerned only with their profits" (Jessop 1986: 40). While wealth is accumulated in fewer hands, producers' basic needs are left unmet.

Our analysis throughout the book reveals that this fundamental contradiction has taken on an even sharper form in the era of the Fourth Industrial Revolution, whose technological effect challenges the limits of modern productive forces themselves. Yet, digital capitalism, by instrumentalizing the 4IR and commodifying data and technology, imposes a strong barrier to the further development of productive forces and, therefore, the entire society. The abundant character of information technologies constitutes a strong marker of this level of development. While capitalist market relations function based on the principle of scarcity, information is rendered abundant in the 4IR era, with the cost of reproducing information goods being reduced towards zero. To counter this tendency, however, digital capitalism resorts to the monopoly power of Big Tech in defence of so-called "intellectual property" (Mason 2015).

Throughout this book, we have discussed the digitalization of capitalism and its manifold implications, as they have taken on a new significance in the face of the COVID-19 pandemic. With the pandemic, we are moving further away from the techno-utopia of digital capitalism encapsulated in the false promises of the 4IR and ever closer to a dystopian future where the technology managed by digital capitalism brings enslavement to our entire lives, as part of today's relations of production. Rather than increasing our free time, improving the quality of our leisure, facilitating our lives, and developing our happiness, the relations of production enforced by digital capitalism turn technology into a tool to intensify exploitation and social control on an unprecedented scale.

At the very heart of Marxism lies the preoccupation that humanity — as "a creature of the very social conditions [s]he himself has created" — has remained "a prisoner of those conditions" (Zeitlin 2001: 145). This preoccupation also applies to technology, as it is instrumentalized under capitalism. During the pandemic, moreover, global capitalism takes advantage of any disastrous vulnerability that may arise, health-wise, economic, or something else, to ensure that the enslaving social conditions of capitalism are left intact. In this manner, the calls for reforming global capitalism in the COVID-19 conjuncture seek to bridge the agenda of further advancing the corporate model of health that is centred on intellectual property (e.g., vaccines supported by corporations, "philanthropic" organization, and states), maximizing the profits of digital monopolies, and advancing the pretext of redressing the ecological crisis for imperialist purposes. If successful, this agenda will serve to create new social conditions that constrain our freedom to realize our human potential to the fullest.

The recent transformations of global capitalism and their implications for society point to the actuality of Marxism as a powerful framework for understanding and changing today's world. A Marxist analysis of today's world of COVID-19 reveals that capitalism has failed to resolve the pandemic crisis in its various forms, all despite the advanced level of development of its productive forces: health emergencies, economic crises, environmental strains, to name a few. This calls for a revolutionary transformation of the relations of production on a more democratic basis, where key policy areas such as labour, the environment, and health are not subjugated to corporate logic any further. A new paradigm is needed, where the productive forces are set free to address the immediate needs of humanity and increase humanity's prospects for self-realization in the process. In Marx's words, this paradigm will gradually pave the way for a world where "all the springs of co-operative wealth flow more abundantly. Only then can the narrow horizon of bourgeois right be crossed in its entirety and society inscribe on its banners: From each according to his ability, to each according to his needs" (Marx 1875). Certainly, the level of development of our productive forces, in particular digital technologies, provide historic opportunities for non-market forms of cooperation and abundance, if they were managed on a humane basis (Mason 2015).

Our entire discussion in this book is devoted to the questions of how the COVID-19 pandemic sharpens the contradictions of global capitalism and affects the future of the capitalist system. But, then, another question that imposes itself next is whether a future without capitalism is attainable. There is room for optimism about such a prospect considering that the pandemic conditions have not sufficed to suppress mass protests such as the Black Lives Matter movement and historic strikes in India. The continued exacerbation of economic circumstances may even lead to conditions that yield revolutionary situations. In such situations, however, mere acts of resistance and escapist strategies focused on creating prefigurative and local alternatives, rather than engaging the state, will certainly fall short of success. In order, therefore, is a postcapitalist strategy of eroding capitalism, which will combine the agenda of building a stronger solidarity economy and state actions by gradually expanding non-market practices. In this transitional program, absolute priority is to be given to a minimum of five key tasks, starting with the tasks of turning information into a public good and suppressing monopoly capital in response to the immediate challenges of digital and surveillance capitalisms. At first sight, these measures evoke the dictatorship of the proletariat, where a popular government gradually introduces "a series of restrictions on the freedom of oppressors, the exploiters, the capitalists... to free humanity from wage slavery" (Lenin 1917). On closer examination, however, suppressing monopolies and their political representatives as well as liberating data from the yoke of corporations and bringing technology to the service of humanity would democratize the society and enable genuine participation and inclusion. At the end of the day, one could argue that suppressing monopolies and liberating data are no more dictatorial than global capitalism restricting access to vaccines, imposing expensive private health services, and forcing the greater mass of underpaid workers into precarious conditions despite their highly intensified workload. Meanwhile, these popular measures are to be supplemented by other tasks that ensure democratization: the introduction of universal basic services, the promotion of solidarity economy, and universal basic income. Concerning the future of capitalism in the post-COVID world, the research agenda of Marxism ahead calls for a "practical-critical" exploration of postcapitalist possibilities in even greater depth (Marx 1845).

REFERENCES

Harnecker, M. 1976. *The Basic Concepts of Historical Materialism.* University of Sydney.

Jessop, B. 1986. "The Future of Capitalism." In R.J. Anderson, J.A. Hughes, W.W. Sharrock (eds.), *Classic Disputes in Sociology* (pp. 36–67). London: Allen and Unwin.

Lenin, V.I. 1917. "The State and Revolution." <https://www.marxists.org/archive/lenin/works/1917/staterev/ch05.htm>.

Marx, K. 1845. "Theses on Feuerbach." <https://www.marxists.org/archive/marx/works/1845/theses/theses.htm>.

____. 1875. "Critique of the Gotha Program." <https://www.marxists.org/archive/marx/works/1875/gotha/ch01.htm>.

Mason, P. 2015. *Postcapitalism: A Guide to Our Future.* London: Allen Lane.

Zeitlin, I.M. 2001. *Ideology and the Development of Sociological Theory.* New Jersey: Prentice-Hall.

Index